Bible Study Can Be Exciting!

Bible Study Can Be Exciting!

A Handbook for Small-Group Bible Study

by
MARY H. GARVIN

Foreword by Rosalind Rinker

ZONDERVAN
PUBLISHING HOUSE

OF THE ZONDERVAN CORPORATION | GRAND RAPIDS, MICHIGAN 49506

Bible Study Can Be Exciting!
Copyright © 1976 by The Zondervan Corporation
Grand Rapids, Michigan

Second printing   1979

Library of Congress Cataloging in Publication Data
Garvin, Mary H
    Bible study can be exciting!

    Bibliography: p.
    1. Bible — Study.   I. Title.
BS600.2.G37   220'.07   75-43816
ISBN 0-310-24911-2

Printed in the United States of America

*To
the people of God
with love*

Contents

Foreword

I first met Mary Garvin in 1969 when my sister, Denise Adler, and I were invited to hold conferences in Taiwan for both missionary and military women. Mary immediately picked up our material and began to study and pray with three friends. In one year's time, ten women from this growing group have worked out a plan for reaching other women through prayer and Bible study in their respective churches and communities.

It was from this small beginning that requests began to pour in. Mary first prepared it for translation into Chinese by the Canadian Presbyterian Church in Taiwan, under which she and her husband serve. The National Women's Committee of the General Assembly published it and have been using it as program material for the past five years.

Because the program was widely used and had sparked renewal in both individuals and groups, missionaries of various denominations became interested. To meet the demand for an English counterpart, they photo-offset a thousand copies. The Lutherans (ALC) in Ontario invited Mary to conduct two area workshops for clergy and lay-leaders, which then became part of their Key 73 emphasis.

Personally, I am delighted with the contents, finding how the Holy Spirit has taught Mary many of the same things He taught me, but in a fresh way. She wrote to me that receiving this teaching had changed her whole life.

I predict that you, too, will be receiving fresh insights as this material begins to illuminate your own mind regarding your own particular group or church. It is Mary Garvin's first book, and because it combines love and practice, I know you will want a copy for yourself, one for your pastor, and one for your church library.

ROSALIND RINKER

California

Preface

"Surely there must be more to being a Christian than just going to church on Sunday! What does being a Christian really mean?"

or

"Bible study? Oh yes! We have a Bible study every week in our church. The minister leads it. We learn some interesting things about the Bible, but it's not too well attended."

or

"But the Bible doesn't seem very relevant to our needs today. It might have meant something to people a long time ago, but I don't see how it says anything to us."

Comments and questions like these, coming from many laypeople today prompted some of us to make some experiments in small-group Bible study. Within the bounds of this small heterogeneous group we sought to discover what it really means to be Christians together. In actuality, we discovered what it means to be the Church. The excitement of this discovery brought challenge, strength, and joy into the lives of that group. Because we wanted to share the experience with other Christians, I began to record what we were learning together. Since we began our experiment five years ago, literally hundreds of people here in Taiwan, and at home in Canada where we spent a one-year furlough, have been influenced by it. The encouragement that I received from so many who have participated challenged me to set it down for others.

The methods described are not new, but I have been amazed to discover that they are not well known to a large majority of ordinary laypeople. They are simple, and the whole group will learn quickly how to use them. Experienced leaders are not necessary. In fact, leadership should rotate so that everyone has opportunity to lead a study.

A minimum of resource materials are required: pencils, paper, Bibles, and open minds and hearts. A Bible dictionary and commentaries would be most helpful, of course, but the unavailability of such is no excuse for not studying the Bible. Your local bookstore can supply you with resource books.

Your minister may often be able to answer questions that the group cannot.

It is my hope that this book will lead you, the reader, into a whole new adventure in Christian living, and that perhaps it will be used in some small way to assist in bringing renewal to the church.

Acknowledgments

I wish to thank the many authors of recent years who, by expressing their own faith in the church as a redemptive agent in God's world, have encouraged me to be an active member of it. They provided much of the impetus for all the experimenting that forms the basis for this book

Lucy Noordhoff, Lucille Hanson, Betty Mayo, and my husband, Murray, read the manuscript in part or whole and advised and encouraged. Cary Whallon did all the typing. God bless them, each one! Countless others encouraged and prayed. Perhaps most important to thank are the many Taiwanese women, and especially Mrs. Chun-Jean Lee, who worked with me in the beginnings of this Bible study program in Taiwan.

To my husband, Murray, and our five children, I can never sufficiently express my gratitude. They have been patient and understanding when meals were late, encouraging when the task of writing bogged down, cooperative when I needed a little extra time for writing, and always supportive.

Rosalind Rinker, author of *Communicating Love Through Prayer*, introduced me to the joy of conversational prayer and small groups when she visited Taiwan in 1969. I shall always be grateful to her for a ministry that changed the whole direction of my life.

The Bible study methods introduced here are from various sources. I am indebted to the following:

The YMCA of Sweden for the Swedish Method, which we have adapted to suit our own patterns;

The Youth Committee of the Church of Scotland, which published *Chart for Adventure* (Edinburgh, 1962), from which we adapted the Head, Heart, and Hand Method, and the Eight Questions Method;

Christian Outreach, Inc., of Huntingdon Valley, Pennsylvania, which published *Growth by Groups* by Lyman Coleman (1965, 1967), from which we adapted the Paraphrase Method;

The Navigators, Colorado Springs, Colorado, who first introduced the Search the Scriptures Method;

Tamiko Nakamura, who introduced us to the Interview Method.

1

Goals in a Small-Group Bible Study

We live in a fragmented world. Broken relationships prevail between nations, between governing and governed, in marriage, in the family, within ourselves. More than ever before, man is asking, "Who am I? Why am I here? Is life some colossal joke? Is it just a game in which man is destined to be the loser?" Overpopulation, pollution, the potential of the weapons we build, and the violence of our own hatred threaten to extinguish us. Loneliness has become the big word of our age. We are cut off from God, if there really is a God; we are cut off from each other, and we are even cut off from ourselves. We hate what we are and what we do. Yet we have no power to be what we know in our hearts we should be. What is the answer?

Who Are We?

As Christians, we believe we have the answer to man's dilemma. Who are we? The Bible tells us in 1 Peter 2:9,10, "You are a chosen race, a royal priesthood, a holy nation, God's own people, that you may declare the wonderful deeds of him who called you out of darkness into his marvelous light. Once you were no people but now you are God's people. Once you had not received mercy but now you have received mercy."

Who are we? We are "God's own people." Once we were like all the other people in our world today: we didn't know who we were, or where we were going, or why. But God's mercy was revealed to us, and we discovered that we are God's people. We have a purpose in life, because we are united with God's great purpose that *all* men should be called His people; that every man should know who he is, whence he came, and where he is going.

The People of God With a Message

How did we come to receive God's mercy?

We cannot receive what we do not know about. That is why communication words are so much a part of the life and message of the Christian Church. We use the words *witness to, tell forth, proclaim.* John says that "in the beginning was the Word, and the Word was with God, and the Word was God" (John 1:1). The message, or the word of God to us, is that God has made us in His own image and for His own purposes. In Jesus Christ He has redeemed us so that His purposes might still be fulfilled. Jesus Christ Himself is the Word that God sends. Jesus Christ says, "Look at Me. This is what God is like. This is what God intended you to be like. Let Me live in you, and your life will have meaning and purpose. In Me there is forgiveness and acceptance. With Me you will not be lonely."

And this is the message that the people of God are called to proclaim: a message of redemption, of purpose, of hope. How can we proclaim it, if we do not know it? And in the answer to that question lies the first goal of a small-group Bible-study program: *To discover what the Word of God is for us today, through the study of the Scriptures.*

The Bible has proved itself to be the Word of God, because down through the ages, through the power of the Holy Spirit, it has spoken to and changed the hearts of men. But on this very fact hinges an important truth. Unless we *allow* the Spirit of God to make the truths of the Scripture *real* in our daily living and relationship with God, ourselves, and other people, the Bible is just another book for us. It has great potential power, just as a large, dammed water reservoir has a great potential supply of electrical power; but unless the floodgates are opened, the water released, and the energy harnessed, that potential electricity won't illumine even one tiny light bulb. So it is with the Bible. Unless we open it with purpose, with hearts seeking to know the truth, and with a willingness to let the Spirit of God use it in our lives, we will find neither redemption nor hope, either for ourselves or for the rest of the world.

The Body of Christ

Another answer the Bible gives the Christian to the question "Who are we?" is found in 1 Corinthians 12:27. Paul summarized the chapter with these words: "All of you, then, are Christ's body, and each one is a part of it" (TEV).

The church is the "body of Christ." It is a *living* body. It is dynamic, it grows, it acts. It is not bound to a rigid form. Just as the human body must be fed and must distribute blood to all its parts in order to nourish them, so must the church, the body of Christ, always provide for Christian nurture so that all its parts are nourished and fed and useful to the whole organism.

This picture that Paul gives of the church is a truly meaningful one. We all have had the experience of a toothache or a backache making us practically useless even though the rest of our body was strong. The church is also weakened by its weakest members. The *head* of the church — or we can say, the dynamics, the personality, the life-controlling factor of the church — is Jesus Christ. A hand that does not receive the message impulses sent out by the brain is a useless hand and a burden to the rest of the body. If Christians do not receive the messages that Christ is transmitting to them, they too become useless and a burden to the church.

The second goal of a small-group Bible study program is, therefore, *to provide for the nurture and spiritual growth of the group members so that they may be enabled to share, by word and deed, the good news of God's redeeming love for all human beings, and indeed, for all that He has created.*

The Fellowship of the Holy Spirit

Human beings are never redeemed in a vacuum. God's redeeming love is meant not only to restore our individual relationships to Him, but also to restore our relationships with each other. Just as God by His Holy Spirit convicts us of our need to be brought into a right relationship with Himself, so does His Spirit work in us to convict us of our needs to be brought into right relationships with our fellowmen and ourselves.

But in fact, how does God bring about the actual redemption or restoration? Being convicted of our need only makes us miserable. How does God finish this work? As one young lady put it, "But *how* can I love someone whom I don't like?" The answer, of course, is "We can't." We can't be redeemed just because we *will* to be. We are redeemed by the death of Jesus Christ on the cross at Calvary. And we cannot be reconciled to our fellowmen, or to ourselves, by *willing* to be. We are reconciled in these relationships, too, by Jesus Christ. But this time, it is the *life* of Jesus Christ in us that reconciles us to one another. As He lives in us (and He does live in all who believe in Him — see John 15; Ephesians 3:14-21; Galatians 2:20; Philippians 1:21; Colossians 1:24-28, especially v. 27; 3:1-4), it is His Spirit who does the loving, the forgiving, the reconciling. Thus those who call themselves Christians, i.e., the church, are often referred to as "the fellowship of the Spirit." The church is those men and women in whom Christ, by His Spirit, lives and through whom He ministers to the present-day needs of mankind. This definition of the church, the fellowship of the Holy Spirit, leads us to understand the third goal of small-group Bible study: *To foster an awareness and understanding of Christian community.*

The Family of Christ

A growing child daily learns what it means to be part of a family. He learns concern for his brothers and sisters, obedience to his parents, property rights, sharing, cooperation, and numerous other lessons. He wasn't born with a knowledge of these things. He had to learn them. As Christians, we too have to learn and grow through experience. The church is our family. We are bound together in this common community by the Holy Spirit of God. We must learn to live within it, and at the same time we must learn to live in the world. But our life in the world cannot be separated from that community, because our basic identity comes from it. We are always marked by our relationship with Jesus Christ. It is in this very dilemma that most Christians have their greatest conflicts.

It is not easy to be a Christian in the world. Part of this difficulty arises out of the fact that it is not even easy to be a Christian (in the sense of demonstrating the love of Christ) in the church! I believe it is an *art* that must be *learned*. The community of God, the church, ought to be the training ground for our service to the world. Just as within the relationships of the family we develop confidence in our own personality that enables us to relate as persons to other people, so within the family of God's people we develop confidence in the life of Christ within us that enables us to live redemptively in the world.

The Small Group as a Laboratory

The small-group Bible study is like a laboratory experiment within the church. A scientist conducting an experiment must have controls before he can draw accurate conclusions. The group provides controls in which to experiment in living the Christian life and thus to draw conclusions that enable us to grow in our knowledge and experience of the life of Christ in us.

The number of persons in the group is a control. We learn

to think of the church as individuals, rather than as a great mass of people.

The group members themselves are controls. They remind us of what we've learned and help us carry intentions through to completion.

The main control, of course, is Jesus Christ in the person of the Holy Spirit, present in the group, teaching, directing, chiding, reprimanding, disciplining, loving, forgiving.

The Word of God is the catalyst in small-group Bible study. It is used by the Holy Spirit to alter the relationships within the group. Later we will discuss some of the alterations that can be expected to take place.

Enabling Gifts

To enable her for her task, the Holy Spirit gives gifts to the church, and some of these are listed in 1 Corinthians 12 and in Romans 12:3-8. Paul tells us in Ephesians 4:11-13 that God gave gifts to men "to prepare all God's people for the work of Christian service, to build up the body of Christ" (Today's English Version). The result is a unity in our faith and our knowledge of Christ, and maturity in Him.

It is important for us to remember that all members do not have, and need not have, the same gifts. We need to be open to discovering our own gifts and to helping others discover theirs. Then in unity we can help each other to use those gifts in our churches, in our families, and in our communities. Small-group Bible study is one way of making us aware of the Spirit's working in our midst, helping us to find our gifts, and enabling us actually to function as the Christian Church.

The three goals of this program, then, are as follows:

1. To discover what the Word of God is for us today, through the study of the Scriptures;

2. To provide for the nurture and spiritual growth of the group members so that they may be enabled to share by word and deed the good news of God's redeeming love for all human beings, and indeed, for all that He has created;

3. To foster an awareness and understanding of Christian community.

Evangelism

At this point, someone is bound to ask, "What about evangelism?" Isn't leading people to believe in Jesus Christ a goal of a small-group Bible-study program? I do not believe that evangelism in itself is a goal; it is a part of all three goals. Bringing all men to a knowledge of Jesus Christ is God's purpose and the church's task. Small-group Bible study programs may be a tool used to accomplish that purpose. When a non-Christian is brought into the group, he should come, knowing that within this group he will be trying to discover what God is saying to him. The first word that must be obeyed is "Believe on the Lord Jesus Christ. . . ." For this person, salvation will be a product of the first goal.

Four Emphases

These things having been said, it is important for us to remember that there are four main emphases in this kind of a program. The program is not complete and will not be so productive or effective if any single emphasis is lacking.

1. The first is on *the study of the Bible*. All the methods given in this book have a common approach. Each one provides for individual study of the passage. Then, time is provided for the group members to share and discuss their findings with each other. And finally, a good deal of importance must be placed on group and individual decisions regarding a plan of action arising out of those findings. The Bible becomes the *living* Word of God when we are obedient to its teaching. Much of the blame for statements like "The Bible is irrelevant" can be placed on the fact that we do not spend enough time in deciding *how* to act upon the Word we have received.

2. The second emphasis is on *the group*. The message of redemption in Jesus Christ is a relationship-centered message. Whenever we find ourselves separating that message from

people, we have separated ourselves from the truth.

The kingdom of God is often called the kingdom of right relationships. We must have a right relationship with God through Jesus Christ, a right relationship with ourselves, a right relationship with our brother or neighbor, and a right relationship with the world. The people in the group are important! If within the group we neglect the expressed needs of even one person, we are disobedient to the Word that we study. The "studied word of God" must become the "applied Word of God" if it is to be redemptive. Unapplied, the Bible becomes a judge that condemns rather than redeems.

The group is important because it is the media in which we learn to apply the truths we receive from our study. We learn how to be concerned for someone in trouble, how to love the person we wouldn't perhaps choose to be our friend, how to encourage the person who has failed, how to share the carrying of another's burdens. We learn how to accept God's discipline from others, how to open ourselves to others so that we can accept God's healing through them, and how to accept the love that others would give us.

3. The third emphasis is on *outreach.* Obedience to the revealed Word of God is a keynote in the program. Down through the history of the church, God's word has always been that the church is a servant-people, called to bear the Good News of Jesus Christ to every human being. A Bible study group that is not reaching out is a disobedient group.

Outreach takes two forms. The first is the outreach of the group members into the community. No Christian can have a ministry among the unevangelized if his interpersonal relations are all within Christian circles. There is a danger that Christians draw themselves together into the fellowship of the church and ignore the rest of the world. Small-group Bible studies should encourage people to go out into the world compelled by the love of Christ for that world. The love and support of the group should be an encouragement to each member as he performs his God-given vocation: the Word of

God studied week by week should give him a strong assurance of the power of God that enables him to perform that ministry.

The second form of outreach is in the growth of the group. This program is built on the principle of cell growth. Experience has taught us that where there is no growth, the group may become stagnant and even die. New members are a confirming sign of our concern for others. They bring new unity to the group, because they bring new concerns, problems, and joys with which the group may struggle and to which the Word of God addresses new messages. When the group becomes too large, it is time to divide in order to allow for continued growth and the involvement of more people.

4. This brings us to the fourth emphasis — *leadership training.* This is of the utmost importance if the program is to grow. Obviously groups cannot be divided into new groups if more leaders are not available.

The methods taught in this book are simple; they are easily learned and easily taught. If the programs included are used in the order given, every member of a group will quickly learn to lead Bible studies using these six methods. In every group there are always "natural leaders," and they will learn more quickly. However, those who are hesitant will need more time and encouragement. The group will need to discipline itself to ensure that these receive as many opportunities to lead as do the natural leaders.

Basic to this emphasis on leadership training is the theory that every group member is a potential leader, because every group member is, or will become, one of God's people who is called out of darkness into His glorious light in order that he may declare the wonderful acts of God.

Summary

1. Goals

(a) The church is God's own people, called to proclaim His wonderful works, and His message to the world. To proclaim the Word we must know what it is, and Bible study is one way of finding out.

(b) The church is the body of Christ, and as such, it must be living and growing. Bible study and obedience to what God reveals in His Word provide the growth that makes us useful, active parts of the body, experiencing and sharing the good news of God's love.

(c) The church is the fellowship of the Holy Spirit. Small-group Bible study programs enable us to experience His power at work in the midst of the group, and this in turn strengthens our faith in, and witness to, the power as it is active in the whole world.

2. Four emphases

(a) The study of the Bible. Obedience to the word God gives releases God's power in the life of the Christian, and thus he becomes a vessel of God's power in the world.

(b) The group. The gospel is about the kingdom of right relationships. The group provides the environment in which we learn to exercise the truths that God has revealed to us, and it makes God's Word vital in our lives.

(c) Outreach. Christians are called to a task, and that task is to proclaim and *live* the gospel message in the world. Failure to reach out to others is disobedience to God's Word and may result in the death of the group. God reveals new messages to those who have obeyed the messages He has already given.

(d) Leadership training. Cell growth — i.e., growth through periodically splitting the group into smaller groups — is possible only if everyone shares responsibility for leadership.

2

How Small-Group Bible Study Can Change Us

Philip A. Anderson, in his book *Church Meetings That Matter*,[1] lists nine changes that are to be expected in a person who actively participates in a Christian group. I shall point out how these nine changes occur through a small-group Bible study experience.

1. "A movement from self-centeredness to care for others."

Our initial reaction in a group includes questions like "Will I fit in? Will the group like me? What do they think of me? Do they care about how I feel?" In a Bible study group we learn to accept ourselves and each other, because we are constantly assured that we belong to God, that He has redeemed us. He forgives us, and so we forgive each other. With assurance, we now begin to ask, "How can I help Bob? Did he feel hurt when the group disagreed with him? How can I show him that I care even though I disagreed too?" Our focus of concern is shifted from ourselves to others.

2. "A movement from doubt about self to trust of self."

We all have different degrees of doubt about our own adequacies. Acceptance by the group of our contributions to its life, and the constant reminder from the Scripture that we are created in the image of God and redeemed to fulfill His intention, help us to discover that each of us is a person of worth and adequacy in Jesus Christ. Assurance of this frees us to participate in greater depth.

3. "A movement from irresponsibility to a sense of responsibility for self and others."

It is impossible to "lose oneself" in a small group. When any one group member is irresponsible, the whole group suffers. In a small group, that suffering is always obvious. A large group always has someone who will be responsible, and the majority of the group can remain silent and inactive without being obviously destructive. In a small group, every member is important, and if one or two people have to carry all the responsibility, the group soon falls apart. The life of the group is dependent on each member's feeling responsible for himself and the other members.

4. "A movement from secrecy to sharing."

There are two ways of practicing secrecy in a group. One way is to keep quiet; the other way is to talk endlessly about questions that are "safe," that do not threaten us. Either way, we are not exposing our true thoughts and feelings to the group. Usually secrecy stems from fear of rejection by the group or from defensiveness. None of us likes to be criticized. But all of us want to be known. I commented once to a friend that I thought people went to cocktail parties in order to get to know other people. "You're wrong!" she replied. "People go to cocktail parties so that other people will get to know them!"

We all yearn for someone to know us as we are and accept us that way. We Christians are free to accept each other as we are, because God accepts us as we are. The Christian group then can encourage authentic sharing and thus meet a basic need found in all human beings.

But sharing must never be for sharing's sake. We must strive for honesty in our sharing. And when someone has opened himself to us, we must ask God for the love and loyalty and sensitivity that will enable us to enter their lives humbly and lovingly, recognizing that this is the ministry to which God has called us and that only Jesus Christ living in us is really capable of carrying it out.

5. "A movement from unfreedom to freedom."

Each of us has things in our lives from which we would like to be free. We would like to be free of our feelings of inadequacy, our frustrations, our need to defend ourselves, our fears of rejection by other people. We would like to be free in sharing our faith, free to serve others, free to admit our failures. But essentially what we all want is freedom to be ourselves.

The problem arises when we ask what we think "we" are. Most of us really want to be perfect. We can accept imperfection, failure, and sin in other people, but we cannot accept it in ourselves. We want to be better than we are, and we want other people to think that we are better than we are too. We are afraid that since we don't like what we really are, other people won't like us either. So we put on false faces. When we do something wrong and are forced to admit it, we say we "lose face." In other words, the false face slips, and people see us as we really are.

Basic to the Christian faith is the doctrine of the forgiveness of sin. We believe that God forgives sin and that because He can forgive what is wrong in us, He is free to really love us, *just as we are!* Because God forgives me and loves me as I really am, I must also forgive myself and love myself as I really am.

When I become part of a group of people who also believe that God has forgiven them, and who have forgiven themselves for not being perfect, I am free to be myself. Why? Because the automatic outcome of this assurance is the ability to forgive and accept *real* people.

The following story demonstrates what I mean. During a small-group Bible study I attended, a young mother was asked to share her paraphrase of a psalm that we were working on. "Before I begin," she said, "there is something I should tell you. I am very angry today, and it will show in the way I've written my paraphrase. I was up all night with a sick child, and I'm tired. I resented having to lose sleep, and I resented my husband sleeping through it all. I am angry with him. I am angry with my child and I am angry with myself!"

I wondered how the group would handle this confession. There were at least three possibilities. We could ignore it, and she would go out of that group feeling that we did not care and wondering if we would tell our friends what an unloving and irresponsible mother she was. (For that was the way she felt about herself.) Or we could criticize her, "Oh, my dear! You shouldn't feel like that! It's your duty as a wife and mother! You *should* be angry at yourself!" And my friend would have gone home feeling guilty and resentful, not just of her husband and child, but of this group that had judged her and had said in effect, if not in words: "You are inadequate. We think we are better than you are. We never experience those attitudes."

Or, the group would respond the third way. One member might say, "Oh, Joan! I know just how you feel! That has happened to me, too. And I always feel so guilty about it!" Another might say, "Yes, me too. What can we do about that guilt and resentment?" Someone else might answer that she found it helpful to thank God for all the joyous things about being a mother, and that helped make the difficult parts seem worth it. Perhaps one member of the group might suggest that they pray for Joan. The prayer would include thankfulness to God that in Jesus Christ we are forgiven for our failures and shortcomings. Someone else might ask God to help Joan to forgive herself, and another might ask God to help all the members in the group to forgive themselves when things like this happen.

This third kind of response would leave Joan feeling that she wasn't alone in her struggle to be a Christian. She would feel understood and accepted. She would not need to defend her wrong attitude. Now she would be free to be *really* herself — not the perfect human being that she set up as a standard for herself, but the forgiven human being who was free to claim

God's help because she had admitted her need.

Unfortunately the group chose not to deal with Joan's frank confession. She left the Bible study that day wishing she had not been so vulnerable, and feeling resentful toward the other women in the group, who had refused to share her burden.

The group is a small section of the church, the people of God. God's Spirit lives in the group. When as members of that group we determine to be honest with each other in the presence of God's Spirit, that same Spirit is there to help us love and accept each other. If we cannot admit our needs and our imperfections to others, then we must erect a wall around us (or put on that "false face"), that will keep others from really knowing the kind of persons we are. As long as that wall is there, we are not free to love or be loved, to forgive or be forgiven, to help or be helped.

A small-group Bible study program helps its members to break out of the chains of fear and guilt, because it provides an environment in which it is relatively safe to be our real selves. When we are free to be ourselves, we no longer need to use our energy in protecting ourselves. We are free to launch out, to serve others, and to love others, and if we fail, the assurance of God's forgiveness and the forgiveness of the group gives us the courage and the freedom to try again.

6. "A movement from mistrust to trust."

In a recent Bible study I asked the group to think for a few minutes about the "darkness" that they had experienced in their lives. Then to share, if possible, something of those experiences and what each person felt had caused the darkness in his life. Immediately one member objected: "What is the use of sharing these things? It doesn't help. In fact, sometimes it makes it worse. The person you share it with can't really understand or help, and besides, you might even share it with a bad person who would betray you." This woman's problem is not uncommon. All of us experience this kind of fear or mistrust of others. A small group provides the environment in which we can experiment with trust. Trust basically is having faith in someone else. As members of Christ's church, our basic faith is in Him, but it must also be faith in Him as He lives in other Christians.

My friend had trouble having faith in others because, as with us all, her trust had probably been betrayed.

Herein lies a problem for the group. Each member is reluctant to trust the group, because he does not know for sure that the group is trustworthy. But it cannot be proved trustworthy unless someone in it is brave enough to test it. If everyone in the group is accepting of the others, uncritical in a judgmental sense, helpful, and truly making an effort to be understanding, a climate of trust is established. Group members move from relationships of acquaintance to relationships of deep friendship. The group feels comfortable. Each member feels that he belongs.

In a trustworthy group, a member feels that he can be his real self, and the group will help him to grow and become the person he really wants to be.

7. "A movement from the need to receive ministry to a concern to give ministry."

The reader will recall that this Bible-study program first arose out of the need that three or four people felt for a kind of study that would help them to grow in their own faith. People were invited to attend the Bible study group on that basis. Members attended for the sake of receiving ministry; they wanted to build up a faith that would work itself out in action in their daily living. One year later, that group of ten women had worked out a plan for reaching other women in their churches and communities. The desire now was to share the ministry they had found with others. This is an example of group growth.

However, growth happens constantly on an individual level. One member of a group came with deep personal needs. For the first meeting or so, she was quiet, observant, testing the group climate, and not contributing a great deal. After having established that the group was trustworthy and really did care about her, she began to share the deep concerns of her heart. As she found her needs being met in the group through study of and obedience to the Word of God, she began to see that others might find the group helpful. So she invited her friends to attend. She began to listen to the expressions of other members' needs, and she was able to pray for them.

Only as the church comes into a real understanding and acceptance of the great ministry that God has performed for her in Jesus Christ will she be able to reach out and minister to the rest of the world.

In a small group, individuals learn how to receive the ministry of Christ and how to minister to others in His name.

8. "A movement from a closed mind to a mind open to learning."

There is great stress today on adult education. Educators are discovering that people learn when they become subjectively involved with the content to be taught, and the whole emphasis in adult education is on participation and involvement.

The Protestant church, with its great historical emphasis on the "Preaching of the Word" finds itself in a giant rut. The emphasis is not wrong; it has simply been too exclusive. The church grew into feeling that the preacher had the Word of God, and the layman had the ears to hear. The result is that the pastor has the awesome responsibility laid on him to be the only one through whom the oracles of God are heard, and the people have felt no call to be temples of the Holy Spirit through whom God works and ministers to His church. The result is frustrated, overworked pastors who have little time to listen to the voice of God, and lazy, uncommitted laymen who sleep either physically or mentally when the Word is preached.

In a small group, no one is allowed to play the "authority role." The participant in the group discovers as people share their struggles and problems that out of his own experience, he is often able to help. He becomes a teacher. But he also discovers that, when he shares himself and his own struggles, others become teachers to him. Because he can share in the teaching process, he becomes a learner.

In the small-group Bible study, even the novice discovers that because he is a person in whom Christ dwells and through whom the Holy Spirit works, he too can contribute to the educational process. Because others take a turn preparing and leading the Bible study, he too takes a turn. Whereas he formerly thought he could only sit and listen to an expert expound the Scriptures, he now finds that he can help to lead the group into a learning experience in which he shares as fully as the rest.

First Peter 2:9, 10 tells us that the church is a royal priesthood called to declare the mighty acts of God. He does not say, "A few of you are chosen." He is talking to all the Christians (1 Peter 1:1) scattered through the provinces. He is talking to every Christian in all times and places. Every Christian is called to be a disciple, a learner of Christ, in order that he may become part of the ministering priesthood. Small-group Bible studies provide a means whereby we become learners of Christ.

9. "A movement from hatred of self, others and God, to a love of self, others and God."

This is the most valuable movement that any person ever makes in a group and, in fact, in his whole life. The world is full of people who hate themselves and, as a result, hate everyone else and God too. Some of these people cover their self-hatred with overly outgoing personalities as they try to prove to themselves that they really *are* nice people. Or, they don't even try to prove it to themselves any more, and we say they have an inferiority complex. The alarming increase in the rate of suicides is proof enough that many people have reached the ultimate in hatred for themselves and are bent on total self-destruction.

One group working with people who attempt, or succeed in committing, suicide in Taiwan, where the suicide rate is high, tells us that the majority of cases are caused by "family problems": unhappy marriages, parent-child relationships. Relationships with other people are the areas in which we most fail. And we hate ourselves when we fail. After we've failed many times, life seems hopeless, and we can no longer face other people. We see only our own failures, and we imagine that they are all other people see too. Others' successes loom large for us and make our failures seem even more obvious. So we begin to hate them too. Our guilt piles up, and we hate God. We hate Him because He made us, and we hate Him because He says we are to love others, and we can't.

This may sound extreme, but it is going on inside us all. What is the answer?

Basically the answer is in forgiveness. None of us ever experiences forgiveness in entirely the same way. Sometimes we experience God's forgiveness in Jesus Christ first. Sometimes we experience His forgiveness through one of His children. But it is only when we experience God's forgiveness, one way or another, that we can begin to forgive ourselves.

Jesus, in that wonderful story in the Gospels (Luke 7:36-50) when the sinner-woman washed His feet with her tears, tells Simon the Pharisee a parable about a man who had two creditors, both of whom he forgave. He asked Simon which creditor would love the man more, the one who owed the great debt or the one who owed the small debt. Of course, Simon answered, "The one whom he forgave more."

When suddenly the wonder of the fact that God does not condemn us, but accepts us as we are; does not come to damn us, but rather to pick us up out of our failure and start us afresh; when suddenly that truth breaks in on us — we are free! We are given hope. God loves us! *God!* The holy, sinless, perfect God *loves* me; just as I am, failure that I am. We have been forgiven much.

And we love Him. When we can say, "I am a failure in the art of living, but God loves me and promises me all His resources to make me a success," then we realize that He can do that for others too, and so can we! Being the church means belonging to a fellowship of forgiven sinners, who receive not only God's forgiveness, but each other's forgiveness too.

In a small group where the chief aim is to study and apply God's Word in our daily living, we learn of God's forgiveness through His Word and through the acceptance and love that members of the group have for each other. We can move from hatred for ourselves, others, and God into a love of self, others, and God.

3

Servant-Leaders/Servant-Members

Leadership Resides in a Function

A basic concept of leadership inherent in our approach to Bible study in small groups is *shared leadership.* It makes the assumption that *leadership resides in a function, not a person.* The elements of this function can be classified into two categories. One category is concerned with achieving task-oriented goals. These elements are —

> Initiation (i.e., "Let's get started")
> Seeking information
> Giving information
> Clarifying
> Elaborating

The second category is concerned with the group and achieving person-oriented goals. We call these the *group-building* or *maintenance* elements. They consist of —

> Encouraging
> Mediating conflicts
> Gate-keeping
> Setting standards
> Relieving tension

In shared leadership, anyone in the group is eligible to provide one or all of these elements as they are needed.

Advantages of Shared Leadership

When we are dealing with adults (and in particular, Christian adults) as we usually are in these programs, we must remember that each person brings to the group his own special gifts, abilities, education, experience, and specific kind of leadership potential. As well, God's Spirit lives in him, enabling him to be a channel of ministry as much as anyone else. Since others in the group are thus capable of assuming the leadership functions, they *may be shared.* In fact, the leadership functions *must be shared* because no *one* person is capable of seeing all the needs.

When leadership is shared, personal investment is higher and group members maintain a more intense loyalty and greater responsibility toward the group. This sense of responsibility is manifested in practical terms in regular and punctual attendance and a greater sense of one's own importance and call to ministry within the group. There will be a more honest and open approach to the Scriptures. A deeper experience of the supportive nature of the group will enable members to respond more readily when those Scriptures reveal the word that God is speaking to them.

Bearing this concept in mind, we may now go on to talk about servant-leaders and servant-members. In John 13:1-17 Jesus Himself demonstrates the meaning of being a servant-leader. His status in the group is not the important thing. Jesus is secure in His knowledge of who He is; He knows that He came from the Father and that He is going to return to the Father. This secure knowledge frees Him to do the thing that is necessary for His group. In this case, their feet needed washing — and apparently no one else was going to do it.

The six methods presented in chapter 4 all call for a servant-leader: someone who will do the practical tasks that have to be done. The responsibilities outlined below are ideally to be shared by every member of the group, and that is the goal toward which every group should strive. But having one person appointed as a kind of moderator (with each member taking a turn) gives the group a feeling of security that is especially needed in the beginning stages.

Responsibilities of the Servant-Leader

1. The servant-leader is familiar with the *passage* to be studied. He has spent time reading it, thinking about it, and praying about it. He has done some research in order to have available the background information about the passage that the group may need.

2. The servant-leader is thoroughly familiar with the *method* he intends to use. He has used it to work through the study passage prior to the meeting of the group.

3. The servant-leader is responsible for *explaining the method* to the group and *getting the study started.* If the method is new, he must explain it in detail; otherwise a simple review is all that is necessary. He is the *timekeeper.* If the method calls for twenty minutes to be spent on discussion, he notes when the twenty minutes has passed and helps the group move on to the next phase of the study.

4. The servant-leader is responsible ultimately for *controlling the discussion.* He is responsible for lovingly and tactfully curbing the members of the group who monopolize the conversation. If the group has previously discussed "Group disciplines" (see page 43), he will need only to remind the overtalkative member of his responsibility.

As well as curbing those who talk too much, the servant-leader is ultimately responsible for *encouraging those who say little* or nothing. I say "ultimately responsible," because the group members themselves all play a part in making each other responsible participants. The servant-leader must be very sensitive to the feelings in the group, and when he observes that it is neglecting the needs of any of its members, he must make the group aware of this failure.

5. The servant-leader is *not an authority*. If the method calls for the leader to introduce the passage to be studied, the introduction should be brief and functional. He has previously prepared and has resources on hand, but if he displays all these resources at once (i.e., if he tells the group everything he has learned as he prepared the study), the group will be overwhelmed and feel they have nothing to contribute. The leader must provide the resources as they are needed and called for.

The less obvious the servant-leader is in this kind of group study, the more successful he is as a leader. Since each member of the group is called to be a responsible participant, the servant-leader should depend on the others to help him in his leadership responsibilities.

6. A servant-leader is *open* and *honest*. A leader can do much to set the atmosphere for a study. If he gives the impression that he has all the answers, he will find the group very unresponsive. If, however, he is open to the ideas of the group, members will more likely express their honest feelings. Often he may have to express his own honest feelings and questions first for the group to feel free to discuss what they are really concerned about.

7. The servant-leader is *a servant*. To be a leader is to be vulnerable — to be in a place where one can easily be hurt. Usually the hurts that come are the results of our own desire to be honored instead of to serve others. A good leader makes other people into leaders. Making leaders out of others means we have to be willing to have others receive honor while we stand at the side and cheer them on, enabling them to do great things. That is hard for all of us, but this is what Jesus meant when He said we should be servants of all. This kind of Bible study program, which is constantly growing and requiring new leaders, is dependent on the servant-leader and shared-leadership concepts.

Responsibilities of the Group

Just as the person who has responsibility at a given time to be "the leader" or "moderator" must think of himself as a servant-leader, so must each member of the group see himself as a servant-member. Each member is called to be a *responsible* participant. What does that mean? To whom is he responsible? For what is he responsible?

If we think in terms of the four emphases of this program, we see that each member is responsible to participate in —

> The Bible study
> The life of the group
> Outreach
> Leadership

1. To be a *responsible* participant *in Bible study* means that every member of the group will come with an honest desire to know what the Bible is saying to him, and with an open willingness at least to try to be obedient to that revealed Word. He will remember that God speaks His Word, not only through the Scriptures, but through His Holy Spirit, who is at work in the members of the group. Because of that, he will be attentive to what the other group members have to say, and he will realize that if God gives him an insight, it is to be shared with the others, not simply stored up in his own mind. If there is something about the Word, or its application, that he does not accept or understand, he has a responsibility to make that known, in order that the group, as the fellowship of the Holy Spirit, might help him to understand.

If someone else has a question, the responsible servant-member who has found an answer will humbly share his experience with the hope that it will be helpful. He will submit all his contributions to the scrutiny of God's Word and His Holy Spirit in an effort to find real truth. Someone has made the accusation that discussion groups are often just "the pooling of ignorance." The responsible participant honestly attempts to contribute helpfully to the discussion.

2. Second, the servant-member is responsible *to the group*. Remember who this group is: the body of Christ. Each

member is beloved of Christ, and all are called to love each other.

Sin has brought separation from God and separation from each other.

Consequently all human beings wear masks. These masks protect us, because they enable us to act acceptable roles in our relationships with other people, thus hiding what we really are and sparing us from their criticism, condemnation, and rejection.

In Christ, however, we are free to be our real selves, to take off our masks, because we are a forgiven, redeemed people. God is already doing a "new thing" in us, already re-creating us in His image. He loves us. Therefore we need not fear the criticism and rejection of others.

But on the other side of this fact lies a responsibility to be a useful member of the body in which Christ still lives and continues to carry out His redeeming activity. This means that we can no longer criticize, condemn, or reject others when they expose their real selves to us. Instead we become channels through which Christ is constantly loving, redeeming, re-creating others.

> Having been forgiven, we are able to forgive.
> Having been loved, we are able to love.
> Having been healed, we are channels for healing.

In Ephesians 4:15, 16 Paul says that in speaking the truth in love, we grow up in every way into Christ. This is the goal of meeting as small groups. We want to become mature in the faith, usable channels of God's grace. God has given different gifts and functions to all the various members of Christ's body. The small group makes it possible for every member of Christ to fulfill those functions and use those gifts that are given for the mutual strengthening and upbuilding of His church.

Some of the key words in a small-group program are —

> Love
>
> Openness (willingness to share and willingness to receive)

Honesty
Confession
Participation
Trust
Trustworthiness
Acceptance
Forgiveness
Healing
Listening
Growth

As Christ lives today in the midst of His people by His Holy Spirit, all that He is capable of doing is available to us today. Matthew 7:7-11 or Luke 11:9-13 tells us that all we need to do is ask. He is longing to do these things for us, even now.

Here in this group, where Jesus lives, He can forgive us, heal us, cleanse us, renew us, empower us, love us, re-create us, and restore our broken relationships. Whatever our need, Christ lives in this group of which we are a part. If we study the list of key words and give ourselves to them, with the assurance that Christ is in our midst, He will do for us all that we desire and, more important, all that He desires.

Let us not be afraid to strip off our masks and be honest within our small group. Let us not be too proud to let Christ minister to us through another member of His body to whom He is the source of Life. Let us not be too selfish to let Christ minister to others through us.

"Beloved, if God so loved us, we also ought to love one another. No man has ever seen God; if we love one another, God abides in us and His love is perfected in us" (1 John 4:11, 12).

Another word to remember as regards the responsibility of each member is *unity*. Because the group is the body of Christ, each member is responsible to help achieve and maintain unity. This unity will arise out of the group's common love for Jesus Christ and for each other.

In practical terms, this means that each member out of love for the others will be honest in sharing his opinions, questions, and feelings. He will know that the group loves him as he is, because Christ loves him as he is. He will remember that all the members have needs to share, and therefore he will not knowingly monopolize all the time or discussion. If he unknowingly does so and another member of the group points this out to him, he will accept the reminder in love. Similarly he will be responsible lovingly to remind other members of the group who fall into the same error.

Out of love and concern for the group, the responsible member will *attend group meetings on time*, and if he cannot, he will inform the group of his difficulty so that they may feel free to start without him.

The responsible participant will remember his role as a servant-member. In all his group relationships, he will do his best to observe the disciplines that the group has set for itself.

3. The third area of responsibility is *outreach*, and again this falls into two categories. Each member will attempt to take the truths that God reveals to him out into the community in which he lives. He will honestly seek for God's guidance in all his relationships whether family, church, work, or society. He will share the good news of God's love with others, both in his activities and in his words. Thus he will help fulfill the purpose of the church.

Besides carrying the Good News out to others, he will seek to bring others into the life of the group, by inviting friends and acquaintances to become part of the Bible study program.

4. The fourth sphere of responsibility is *leadership*. The importance of ongoing leadership training within the program has already been discussed. Each servant-member must recognize his potential as a servant-leader. If the group reaches out and new members are constantly brought in; if the methods suggested for use are to be most effective; and if each member of the group is to continue to feel that his contribution to the life

of the group is important — the group must be prepared to divide periodically.

The recommended number of members per group is between five and ten. If a group numbers more than seven, it should divide in two for discussion periods. Otherwise it will be difficult to stay within the time limits the group has set.

Every member is a potential leader who may one day carry responsibility for training others. To some, this fact may be frightening. It need not be. No one who is unready to carry leadership responsibility should be forced into doing so. At the same time, most people discover that by the end of five months in the program, they are capable of serving as a leader, because the whole group is there to assist them in this function.

In the light of these four areas of responsibility, the group members should seek to adopt a few personal disciplines. The following suggestions may prove helpful. This contract can be used profitably as written, but it is the group's privilege to alter it.

As a member, I agree to —

- — Attend every week except in the case of emergency;

- — Spend at least twenty minutes daily in regular Bible reading and prayer;

- — Observe time boundaries set on meetings (punctuality in both beginning and closing);

- — Practice submitting every decision in my life to God, honestly seeking His direction in my life through prayer and study of the Scriptures;

- — Participate as fully as it is possible for me in the life and responsibilities of the group.

Summary

Leadership concepts in the small-group Bible study program include —

Shared leadership
Servant-leader
Servant-member
Observance of group disciplines

4

Evaluation/Roadmap to Group-Process Improvement

Evaluation

Periodic evaluation is important to the growth and life of the group. It not only enables the group to see where it is failing so that changes can be made, but may also prevent stagnation by providing guidelines for successful group life. It may be done by individuals or by the group as a whole.

There are many different ways of evaluating a program, of course, but for simplicity's sake here is a set of questions for the servant-leader, a set for the group members to help evaluate individual performance, and an evaluation from which may be used by the whole group to evaluate the group process.

1. For the Bible study leader:

(a) Does each group member really become involved in the study (i.e., Is each member of the group interested in what is being said, or is there someone in the group who is bored or feels "shut out" of the group?)?

(b) Does each person really understand the aims of the group?

(c) Does the study change attitudes, ambitions, or actions?

(d) Do I learn with the group?

(e) Are members really listening (or searching) for the Word of God?

(f) Does the Bible study involve some activity?

(g) Is the study informal?

(h) Are the members stimulated to do further study?[1]

2. For the group members

This set of questions is taken from *Learning Together in Christian Fellowship* by Sara Little.[2]

(a) Did I prepare before I came, both by prayer and by study?

(b) Did I really try to listen to every person and understand exactly what he was saying?

(c) Did I monopolize conversation? Or, when I spoke, did I have something relevant to contribute or a question to ask that helped us move along in our thinking?

(d) Did I make any effort to help when I saw something was needed, either a question or a fact or a response to some person? Or did I just feel critical and do nothing?

(e) Was I honest? Or did I say what I thought the group expected?

(f) Did I make an effort to think and speak clearly and to listen to others expectantly, believing that God can and does speak to us through one another?

(g) Am I willing to follow through on implications for myself on any truth I glimpsed? Or do I see only what it means for someone else?

3. Small Group Evaluation Sheet[3]

IN THIS MEETING (Circle one category for each statement.)

1. LEADERSHIP WAS	Dominated by one person	Dominated by a subgroup	Centered in about half the group	Shared by all members of group
2. COMMUNICATION WAS	Badly blocked	Difficult	Fairly open	Very open and free-flowing
3. PEOPLE WERE	Phony	Hidden	Fairly open	Honest and authentic
4. THE GROUP WAS	Avoiding its task	Loafing	Getting some work done	Working hard at its task
5. I FELT	Misunderstood and rejected	Somewhat misunderstood	Somewhat accepted	Completely accepted and understood by the group

6. The one word that I would use to describe the climate of this meeting is ____________________.

7. Suggestions:

Dangers

It would be unfair in a discussion of small-group Bible study programs not to warn participants of the dangers involved. All of them can be traced to human weakness, and all can be prevented if the group is aware that they exist and is willing to prevent them.

1. There is a danger of *subjectivism*. This happens when the group becomes too occupied with its own problems to the exclusion of problems not directly related to the group, particularly of the community and the world.

2. There is a danger of *sentimentalism*, a twofold problem. The first aspect has to do with the group's attitude toward the Word of God. If the members spend most of their time *talking* about the precious truths of the Bible and Christian experience and do not apply these truths to their daily lives and God's task in the world, the group has lost its usefulness. Such activity may be pleasant for a while, but eventually the group will lose its sense of purpose, and members will become restless or simply drop out.

The other aspect of sentimentalism has to do with the composition of the group itself. This danger is a common one, especially among Christians who have never before experienced the real meaning of belonging to the fellowship of the Holy Spirit. When suddenly the wonder of this breaks in upon the group, they experience such a love and concern and fellowship with one another that they are reluctant to add new people or to divide the group. I do not think this can be prevented entirely. But the group must overcome it. This can be accomplished only as the members remain open to the Holy Spirit and in faith step out and do the required thing, which is to invite newcomers or divide. One experience of this will immunize each member against its becoming an obstacle again, for each one will discover that every new group is more exciting than the last and just as much a fellowship of the Holy Spirit.

3. There is a danger of *spiritual pride*. Any group that

begins to criticize other Christians who seem less interested in what they consider vital will automatically cut itself off from being able to minister to, or receive ministry from, others of Christ's body. Honest response to the Word of God will prevent this danger.

With God there are no favorites. He wants to be as real and powerful in the life of one Christian as in another. When Christian groups set up their own "rules of spirituality," they cease to listen to God's Word and Spirit. They are like the salt that has lost its taste (Matthew 5:13) and is no longer good for anything.

4. There is a danger of *self-sufficiency*. Beware that the group meeting does not take the place of Sunday worship or the larger fellowship of the organized body of Christ. When a group withdraws from these relationships, it also tends to withdraw from a sense of community responsibility. Keeping the commands of Christ to preach the gospel to every creature and to minister to the needs of all men; all Paul's admonishments to meet with others for public worship, to bear one another's burdens — these should help the group to avoid the pitfall of self-sufficiency. As long as the group takes seriously its charge to reach out and train others, it will never feel self-sufficient.

5. There is a danger of *aceticism*. When the group begins to spiritualize everything and ignore or withdraw from confrontations with the practical, everyday problems of life, the Spirit of God will no longer be free to use its members as a redemptive power in His world.

6. There is a danger of *heresy*. This program has been developed for laypeople who have no special training in understanding the Scriptures. As such, the group can more easily be led into misunderstanding. However, dangerous as this may seem, the value of getting laymen to study God's Word and apply it to their lives far outweighs the danger.

Heresy can be prevented if the group, in its studies, tries to relate every single thing it reads in the Scripture to the gospel as a whole. It can be prevented if the group, whenever a dispute over meaning arises, will find an authority (their minister or a reputable book) who can enlighten them. And finally, heresy can be prevented if the group remains open to the testimony and teaching of the Holy Spirit.

In summary, let us remember —

1. Evaluation is a useful tool for helping us to arrive at our desired goal.

2. Small-group programs have potential dangers. We can prevent these dangers from becoming realities if we are open to the leading of God's Spirit in our individual lives and in the life of the group, through the ministry and teaching of the Scriptures and the church.

5

Six Bible Study Methods

The Bible study methods that we introduce here are not new, and they represent only a handful of the many that are used in studying God's Word.

These particular methods have been chosen for several reasons. They are simple — easy to learn and easy to use. They require participation from the whole group, and they encourage a personal individual study of the Scriptures. They emphasize the importance of practical application, not only in the life of the individual, but in the life of the church, the community, and the world.

It has not been possible to trace the origins of all. Some of the methods have been adapted to better suit the principles on which this particular program is based.

Experienced students of the Bible may feel somewhat hampered by the methods when the group first begins to use them. It will seem at times as though more energy is spent learning the method than in studying the Bible. Do not let that discourage you! Learning the methods well will pay great dividends. Those who master them will soon discover a freedom to use them as very helpful tools, not only in group study, but for personal Bible study too. They are to be thought of, not as bars which restrict the group, but as a door which opens into exciting new adventures in the kingdom of God.

But here must come a word of advice. A group can do no better than to insist that they follow the guidelines given for using a method until every member is thoroughly familiar with it.

Each of the six methods uses a different approach to the passage of Scripture to be studied, but all require an answer in some form or other to the following four questions:

1. What does the passage say?
2. What does the passage say to me?
3. What am I going to do about it?
4. How can the group help me?

Traditional Bible study for most of us has consisted in answering only the first two questions — which probably accounts in part for the common protest that "Bible study isn't relevant." Having left the responsibility of teaching the Bible in the hands of the preachers and teachers, we have heard a good deal about what the Bible *contains*. However, while such persons may be adept at explaining the content of Scripture, they are limited considerably in interpreting it to individuals by the fact that they often are not aware of the circumstances and problems of their listeners' lives. As a result, the application of Scripture to life becomes a generalization, and people are much less likely to go on to even *asking* the third question, let alone *answering* it.

This is not to say that "preaching" does not have its place. Paul tells us in Romans 10:17, "So faith comes from what is heard, and what is heard comes by the preaching of Christ." We all know that the Spirit of God has mightily used preaching as a method of reaching men with the gospel.

It is to say, however, that a person can be greatly helped to see the relevance of the gospel to his own need through small-group Bible study.

The fourth question, "How can the group help me?" has rarely been asked in traditional Bible study groups. This may have been due to the size of the group, the kind of leadership used, or the fact that the group members did not know each other well enough to ask favors of one another.

To understand what kind of answers we are looking for when we ask these questions, let us consider each separately.

1. What does the passage say?

In discovering God's message for us today, it is important that we understand the context in which the Bible was originally written. Everyone with serious intention to study it should try to read something about how the Bible came into being and was finally put together.[1] Perhaps you could invite your pastor to talk to the group about the origin and history of biblical literature. Your church or public library will contain useful resources.

Besides understanding the context in which the Bible as a whole was given to us, it is important to understand the context of the particular passage you will study. The book containing the passage will give insight, and you will benefit from reading a commentary on the passage. Try to discover the meaning of unfamiliar words or cultural concepts or customs that are strange to you. Are the worship forms different from those we observe today? In what way?

Then, too, it is important to know what kind of people the passage was written for. What were their circumstances? Were they believers or unbelievers? Under persecution? Disobedient? Old? Young? Rich? Poor? In other words, what is the situation into which God sent His message? What are the circumstances to which it applied?

2. What does the passage say to me?

This is the question that begins to make us see the relevancy of God's Word. Before we can answer it, there will have to be for each individual an honest recognition of his needs, gifts, and circumstances. We will have to be willing not only to *recognize* the truth about ourselves, but to *admit* to it. We will have to be willing to think honestly about our relationships with other people. Then we will have to apply God's Word to those circumstances, needs, and relationships.

This act of application involves a realization that God's Word is not static. It is a living word. Whenever the same principles are involved, God speaks to us through His Word today just as He spoke to His people centuries ago. And as it did then, so now God's Word demands a decision on our part. To hear God speaking requires that we do something about what He says. That is why we ask the next question.

3. What am I going to do about it?

Abroad in the church is a commonly held misconception (though few of us, if any, will admit to holding it!) that when God speaks to us, there is thunder and lightning, or else some mystical feeling of peace or joy. When we answer, there is bound to be more lightning, accompanied by fantastic, outstandingly obvious changes in personal character.

This idea, ridiculous as it may seem to you, has a subtle but important influence on the rate of our spiritual growth. It usually results in functional deafness of our spiritual ears, and we miss hearing what God is saying to us about the little things (as we call them) in our lives. When God speaks to us, it may concern something big or something little by our standards. But God's standard for us is Jesus Christ. His plan is that we should be changed into His likeness — and everything in our lives that hinders that process is important to Him. The decision we make concerning what God says to us in His Word may seem a very small thing, or a very big thing, but if we do not carry through with it, we are standing in the way of God's purpose for us.

Jesus tells us in John 14:23, "If a man loves me, he will keep my word, and my Father will love him, and we will come to him and make our home with him." Bible study that does not result in a practical working-out of God's message is only half-finished.

4. How can the group help me?

Before the group can help any of its members to carry through on a decision he has made, they must know what the decision is.

Sharing something as personal as a decision about our lives and the way we live them in relation to God, other people, and things, is not easy. But when we find the courage to share this with others, we discover a new resource for growth. The first way the group can help is by *just listening.* Lyman Coleman suggests four tips for the group to keep in mind when a person "decides to let the others in on his life."

First, don't interrupt.
Second, don't probe.
Third, don't give advice.
Fourth, don't judge.[2]

Just listen.

This kind of honest sharing in a loving and trustworthy group will result in discovering what it really means to be part of the community of faith. Much Scripture lends support to this community experience. We are told to bear one another's burdens, and so fulfill the law of Christ" (Galatians 6:2); to "be servants of one another" (Galatians 5:13). Romans 15:1,2 talks about the strong bearing with the failures of the weak. The whole concept of the church's being the body of Christ implies interdependence of Christians upon one another for growth, support, and nurture.

As well as listening to one another, the group becomes the agent through which Christ expresses His love for each person. This love is evident in the genuine concern the group shows, not only in the way its members listen, but also in the practical action they take. I recall once when, as a pastor's wife with five young children and a hectic schedule, I expressed to a Bible study group my fatigue and my need to sort out priorities. I asked them to pray for me, and that was all I expected or desired. But next morning, one of the ladies arrived on the doorstep with her apron. In an authoritative tone of voice she announced her intention to do the ironing — and iron she did, despite my prideful protests! I had no doubt of her loving concern for me!

Having once shared our need with the group, we have several concerned memories to draw on, and this can be very helpful in holding us to our best intentions.

If the thing God asks us to do is difficult for us, we are prone to forget that He asked or that we decided to do it. Having someone who loves us, who wants to see God's purpose fulfilled in our lives, jogs our memories occasionally and spurs us on to carry out our intention.

Another resource available to us in the group is experience. It is not always wise to give advice on the basis of experience unless we know *all* the facts; but it is helpful to share our own experiences when they relate to a need expressed. Over the years, I have received much encouragement, particularly in family relationships, through the honest sharing of experiences by mothers and wives who were more mature than I.

Prayer is one of the most important kinds of aid a group can give to its members. We can pray for one another in our actual time of meeting, and we can pray for one another constantly through the days between meetings. Chapter 6 deals more fully with the subject of prayer.

On the following pages you encounter six methods of Bible study. The description of each method is followed by an actual Bible study that you may do with your group to demonstrate how to use the method. At the end of this chapter a chart compares the methods and describes the particular usefulness of each. You will find this chart helpful in deciding which method to use when you begin to choose your own passages of Scripture for study.

A. IMAGINATIVE INTERVIEW METHOD

For use in the study of encounters with Jesus Christ recorded in the Gospels.

1. The passage to be studied should be read aloud, either verse by verse around the circle or by one person. Use a modern version.

2. Divide your group into teams of 2 - 4, depending on the number of biblical personalities in the story whom you may want to interview. Each group will center around one story personality. The leader should have chosen the characters and the size of each team before the study period.

Each team will study the passage to gather facts about the person(s) to be interviewed. The interview should reveal (1) who the person is; (2) what happened; and (3) what his reaction was to Jesus.

Possible leading questions are —

> Who are you?
> What do you do?
> Where do you live?
> What happened when you met Jesus?
> What do you think of Him? Who do you think He is?
> What difference is meeting Him going to make in your
>   life?

One member of the team is the interviewer, while the other role-plays the biblical character or characters. The interviewer must be truly curious. The interviewed must try to put himself in the shoes of the person whose role he is playing.

Allow 15 - 20 minutes for the teams to decide what was important in the incident, how they felt, what effect Jesus had on them. The interviewer will prepare a number of questions he believes should be answered in order to inform his audience about what really happened. The interviewee will familiarize himself with the character whose role he is to play, so that he may know how to answer the questions asked him.

3. During the next forty minutes, each team will present their interview (as they would if it were a TV or radio coverage of a news item) to the other members of the group. Each team should know how much time is allowed.

After the presentation, members of the group should be encouraged to comment on new insights prompted by the interviews, to ask questions, and to share any applications to their own lives that arise out of the study of this passage. Teams may want to share some of the discussion that occurred during their preparation.

If your group is unaccustomed to discussion and sharing thoughts, the leader would be wise to have a few key questions prepared to help the group bring forth their ideas. Examples are: "How did you feel in your role? In what way did Jesus treat this person differently than other people treated him?" Note that Jesus' actions are always an example to us of how we may treat others. We may also put ourselves in the place of the main character and know that Jesus will treat us that way too.

Follow this sharing time with prayer.

The Interview Method — Sample

> Study passage: Matthew 14:22-33
> Time: 60 - 75 minutes
> Group size: 5 persons

Step 1. Ask God's Spirit to teach you from His Word and through each other. Read the passage together aloud, each member of the group reading two verses to the end of the passage.

Have one member of the group read the following:

> Notice that Jesus had just heard the news of his cousin John the Baptist's death (14:1-12), and we are told that when Jesus heard the news he went off by himself to a lonely place (v. 13). But the crowds followed Him, and in great compassion He had spent the day ministering to their needs, healing their sick, and then climaxing the day by feeding five thousand men (not counting the women and children!), when all He had to work with was five small loaves and two fishes. Remember that

Peter and the other disciples had seen Jesus do this great thing. In fact, they had helped distribute the food and gather up the leftovers. Consider the effect this must have had on them as you study Matthew 14:22-33.

Step 2. Divide into two teams of two or three persons. Team 1 comprises an Interviewer and two other Disciples. Team 2 comprises an Interviewer and Peter. Decide which of you will play which roles.

Spend fifteen minutes in your two groups discovering the answers to the questions which follow. You may use your imagination only as far as you can base your answers on historical fact — of course, you may use cross references in your Bible. If you are the interviewer, be truly curious; think up some questions on your own. If you are Peter or the other disciples, try to imagine how they would feel; put yourself in their situation, and feel their feelings.

Here are some questions to consider besides your own:

> Who are you?
> Where do you live?
> What do you do?
> How long have you known Jesus?
> What happened out there in the boat tonight?
> How did you feel about it?
> What do you think of Jesus? Who do you think He is?
> Is knowing Him as you do now going to make any difference in your life?

Step 3. After fifteen minutes, reconvene the entire group. Pretend you are on radio or television. Be enthusiastic and conduct your interview for the others, with Team 1 leading off. Limit each interview to 5 - 7 minutes.

After each interview, allow the other team to ask the interviewee questions of its own.

Step 4. Spend fifteen minutes discussing the following questions together:

1. If you had been Peter when Jesus invited him to step

out of the boat and come, how would you have reacted?

2. What particular part of the story "speaks" to your life at this moment?

3. How do you react to taking risks?

4. If you knew you could not fail, what one thing would you like to give yourself to in the immediate future? What are you lacking that keeps you from doing it? — e.g., confidence? faith? sufficient planning? decisiveness? courage? something else?

Join your hands in a circle. Ask one member of your group to call "time" at the end of one minute. During that minute, bow your head and in silence pray for the person on your right, asking God to give him what he needs to "launch out" and do what He wants them to do.

B. SWEDISH METHOD

1. Introduce passage

Who wrote it (epistles), or if it is a narrative, who says it and under what circumstances?
To whom is it written?
Relate any background material that may be useful in understanding the meaning of the story.

2. Pray for the guidance and instruction of the Holy Spirit.

3. Read the passage aloud together.

4. Pass out paper and pencils, and briefly explain the symbols used. Divide each paper into three parts, and draw one symbol on each part.

? Any question you have about the passage, e.g., content, word meanings, or hard sayings.

Those thoughts which, after the passage has been gone over several times, gain new clarity and give insight into the rest of the passage or into your own personal faith and experience.

➤ Anything that convicts your heart, challenges you, or pricks your conscience with its judgment or appeal; a commandment to obey, or a promise to claim.

The four steps described above should not take more than ten minutes altogether.

5. Allow 15 - 20 minutes for each person to read the passage and fill in the sheet of symbols.

6. Share the questions around the circle. Answer only the *fact* questions immediately (e.g., What is a Pharisee?). Record questions concerning content or theology on a blackboard or on paper.

7. Share insights. During steps 7 and 8, allow discussion of things shared. Note whether or not some of the insights shared answer some of the questions asked.

8. Allow five minutes for group members to add anything under the arrow that the discussion has brought to light. Make sure that each member is stimulated to ask himself the question "What am I personally going to do about what I have read?" Share your answers with one another if possible, and discuss how you may help each other to follow through on your decisions.

9. General discussion. Any unanswered questions can be discussed at this time, and if answers do not arise from the group, make plans for finding the answers elsewhere (e.g., from your minister or resource books).

Allow approximately twenty minutes for steps 6 and 7. Allow twenty minutes for steps 8 and 9.

10. *Briefly* sum up main points, and close with prayer.

The Swedish Method — Sample

Study passage: Psalm 51
Time: 75 minutes
Group size: 4 - 7 persons

Step 1. Ask God's Spirit to teach you through His Word and through each other. Read the passage aloud together, each person reading three or four verses to the end.

Have one person read aloud the introduction to the passage as follows:

> This is a psalm of David. It was written after Nathan the prophet had come to David to accuse him of his sin with Bathsheba. The story can be found in 2 Samuel 11:1-12:15. Briefly it is this. King David, having reached a time of religious, political, and economical success in his life, took to himself Bathsheba, the wife of Uriah, one of his soldiers. When he discovered that she was pregnant with his child, he tried to cover his sin by bringing Uriah home from battle. But the plan failed when Uriah refused to go home to his wife, so David arranged for Uriah's death in battle. Then he took Bathsheba to be his wife.
>
> Psalm 51 is the song of David's great sorrow over his sin. It is the cry of any of God's children when the Spirit of God convicts of sin.
>
> (For information on the sacrifices spoken of in verses 16 and 19, look at Leviticus 4-7:10.)

Step 2. Allow fifteen minutes for each person to study the passage silently and individually and to fill in the space under each symbol. Each participant will need a paper divided into three sections, one symbol for each section.

(See pages 60, 61 for an explanation of the symbols and their use.)

Step 3. For twenty minutes go around the circle and share your questions. Answer the fact questions first. List the "idea questions" on a blackboard or piece of paper. Discover whether anyone has the answer to any of these in his candle section. Discuss these briefly.

Continue to share what each one has written under his candle symbol.

Step 4. For five minutes sit quietly and meditate on the passage and what has been said about it. Add to the arrow section of your paper anything new that God is saying to you personally.

Write down one specific thing you are going to do about it, and when.

Step 5. Share your arrows with each other around the circle for twenty minutes. Help each other to understand how forgiveness is possible.

Join hands around the circle and spend one or two minutes in prayer for one another (silent or spoken as your group decides). Ask one person to close the time of prayer.

C. HEAD, HEART, AND HAND METHOD

For any size of group dividing up into smaller groups for discussion if group is larger than seven. Type of passage: almost any in the Old or New Testament.

HEAD. This section deals with the facts of the passage. The leader should be familiar with the passage ahead of time and find out the meaning of difficult words or concepts. He should know, if applicable, who wrote the passage, to whom, and why. His introduction should answer the following questions:

> Meaning of words
> The facts of the story or thought pattern of the passage
> Context
> For whom, to whom, and by whom it was written
> What kind of people they were, and what their needs
> were

First, read the passage through together. Are there any difficult words?

Then have each member write down a brief outline of the passage: perhaps just a title for each paragraph, or a summary of each thought.

Now study each section and try to put in your own words what the writer was saying. Get the essential meaning of each section.

HEART. In this section we try to discover what the *heart* of the passage is for each of us as individuals or as a group.

Have each person read the passage again silently. Each is to ask himself, "What does this mean to me in my own personal situation? Is there something in my life that should change? Am I the kind of person this passage is talking about? What is the most important thing this passage says to me?"

Further questions will rise out of the passage. Have each member write down (for remembering only) what is the heart of the passage for him.

HAND. This is the practical part of this type of study. It is not enough simply to *know* our shortcomings, failures, sins, and needs; we must be willing to do something about them or let God do something about them. By this time in the study, the meaning of the passage is clear and each group member should know what the passage is saying to him as an individual.

At this point invite each member to share what the passage has said to him *and* what he is going to do about it. Is there any way that the group can help him? Maybe by praying for him, or by asking the next time you meet if he has done what he believed God had asked him to do.

Close with conversational prayer.

Each section should take twenty minutes. Do not prolong the study: one hour is sufficient. Remember that the leader's task is to —

> Present background;
> Watch the time;
> See that everyone gets a chance to talk and that no one
>   monopolizes the conversation;
> See that no one in the group is "shut out."

The Head, Heart, and Hand Method — Sample

> Study passage: Colossians 3:9-17
> Time: 60 - 75 minutes
> Group size: 5 - 7 persons

Step 1/ Head. Allow twenty-five minutes for this section, including five minutes for the introduction that follows:

The letter to the Colossians was written by Paul from prison, about A.D. 61. It was written to refute the heresies of Gnosticism. This heresy stood in opposition to the true Christian faith in a number of ways, but for our needs today we note only three.

1. Gnosticism attacked the total adequacy and supremacy of Jesus Christ and added many mediators.

2. Matter was evil and eternal. Therefore the flesh was evil. This Jesus, who came in flesh, could not have been God. Besides doctrine, the ethic of the Gnostic was affected by this belief. Two styles of life resulted:

(a) Antinomianism: the flesh was evil; only the spirit was important. Therefore any immorality was justified.

(b) Asceticism: the body, being evil, was starved, denied, and mistreated in an effort to refuse its every need and desire.

Naturally these attitudes affected their relationships and attitudes toward one another.

3. Great emphasis was placed on intellectual understanding and on attaining new heights of success that progressed toward a real union with God as the end-product. Ritual observances, intellectual exercises, passwords, rules, and secret knowledge were emphasized, resulting in a kind of "class system" or "spiritual elite" among those who sought to know God.

Scripture. This passage may be thought of as a guide for the Christian in matters of relationship with one another. Read the passage aloud (a verse by each person or else one person reading the entire passage).

Now allow twenty minutes for the group to study the passage individually. Break it up into paragraphs or topics.

Give each topic or paragraph a title (or heading). *Then* make brief notes under each heading as to the content of that particular portion. In other words, you have twenty minutes to discover what the writer was saying to the Colossian Christians.

Here is a sample outline.

HEAD

Colossians 3:1-4 — How to know what you're to be

    (a) Seek after spiritual values (things that are above)
    (b) Set your mind on the right priorities
    (c) Christ is your life-source now
    (d) You will share His likeness (glory — all that He is)

5-11 — Get rid of what you were

    (a) Kill, by an act of will, all that is part of the old nature (listed in vv. 5-8)
    (b) They are all part of the old life
    (c) By putting on the "new nature" (v. 10)
    (d) No "line-drawing" here. Christ is all, and in all.

12-17 — How to be what you are now

    (a) Put on "garments of righteousness" — those worn by God's chosen ones; vv. 12, 13 — compassion, kindness, lowliness, meekness, patience, forbearance, forgiveness, love
    (b) Let peace be the ruler in your heart, bringing unity
    (c) Be thankful (vv. 15-17)
    (d) Learn your lines well ("Let the word of Christ dwell in you richly")
    (e) Do whatever you do in the nature and role of Jesus

Step 2/Heart. Allow twenty-five minutes for this section.

For five minutes have each person reread the passage and pick out what is for them, the *heart* of the passage (i.e., What is the Word of God to me particularly?). Write it down concisely.

Allow twenty minutes now to go around the circle twice and

1. Share the *headings* you prepared;
2. Share (on the second round) what God is saying to you (the Heart).

Make sure everyone gets an opportunity to share, and that everyone in the group feels free to ask questions of the group member who is sharing. Use Scripture to back your answers.

Step 3/ Hand. Allow twenty minutes for this section.

Take five minutes for each person to consider quietly how the discussion and the Word relate to him, and what particular attitude or action needs to change in his life as a result of this time of study together.

What specific action is he going to take? Write it down.

For the next 10 - 15 minutes, share your decisions with one another around the circle, expressing how you may need help to carry it out.

Prayer time. Have your group stand, join hands in a circle, and spend 5-10 minutes in conversational prayer for one another to carry out decisions they have made.

Prayers should be *specific* and *brief*. (If you monopolize the time with long prayers, other group members are free to tell you so.)

Be sure that you have prayed for everyone in the group before the servant-leader closes the prayer time.

D. THE EIGHT QUESTIONS METHOD

Purpose. To discover what message the passage has for us personally. We relate it to our own situation and to others in the present world.

Allow sufficient time for a silent individual reading of the passage, or read it aloud together. Then either as a group using a blackboard and chalk, or individually using paper and pencil, answer the following questions:

1. Where and when does this incident take place? (If the passage is from an epistle, find out, if possible, who the writer was and to whom he was writing.)

2. Who are the main characters in the passage?
3. What are the difficult words or phrases?
4. What historical situation lies behind it?
5. What are the main ideas of the passage?
6. What did the passage mean for those to whom it was originally addressed? In answering this question, try to put yourself in the situation of those for whom the words were originally intended. Did these words meet a need?
7. What does this passage say to people today? What elements are common to the original situation and to our present day situation?
8. What is the meaning of the passage for me?

> (a) What change in my own attitude or actions are called for by my study of this passage?
> (b) Am I ready to accept this demand now? What help do I need?

Time division.
1. Questions 1 through 4 may be answered briefly by the leader as an introduction, or the group may answer them together if they have prepared the lesson prior to the meeting time. Allow 5-10 minutes.
2. Questions 5 through 7 should be answered in written form individually. Allow 15-20 minutes for quiet study of the passage.
3. Allow fifteen minutes for discussion and sharing of answers.
4. Allow 5-10 minutes for quiet individual answering of question 8.
5. Allow ten minutes for sharing on answers to question 8. Spend a short time in conversational prayer after the study period.

Eight Questions — Sample

Study passage: Matthew 22:1-14
Time: 60-75 minutes
Group size: 4-7 persons

Step 1. Ask the Holy Spirit to direct your minds and hearts into God's truth, and to teach you through His word, and one another.

Allow 10-15 minutes for Step 1.

Read the passage aloud, taking turns around the circle.

Ask one person to read aloud the answers to questions 1 through 4 given below. (Actually this forms the introduction to the study passage and would normally be prepared before the meeting by the appointed leader for the day.)

1. When, to whom, and by whom was this discourse delivered (or passage written)?

The two parables in this passage were part of a discourse delivered by Jesus Himself to the chief priests and Pharisees, the Jewish religious leaders of the day.

2. Who are the main characters in the story?

They are a king, his servants, the invited guests of the wedding feast, and a man who attended without a wedding garment.

3. What are the difficult words or phrases in the passage?

It was the custom that the invitation for the marriage feast be sent out without a specific time stated. When everything was ready, the servants were sent to gather the guests and bring them to the dinner.

It was customary to wear one's good clothes to the feast. Even now, we dress up for our friends, not because our clothes matter to our friends, but because the way we dress demonstrates respect and affection for them. A guest at the wedding feast was expected to bathe, wear perfumed ointments, and don a special garment to the feast to demonstrate his esteem for the host.

4. What historical situation lies behind the passage?

Matthew places this story in Holy Week. Jesus has already ridden into Jerusalem on a colt, proclaiming His Messiahship. The Jews expect the Messiah to be a mighty political leader who will bring in the kingdom of heaven. Jesus has also just recently cleansed the temple.

Now the Jewish leaders are questioning His authority. He says He is the King — the Messiah. They want to know if He comes from God. Jesus' answer to them is in parables, and through these stories He is telling them that they have a wrong concept of the kingdom of God.

Step 2. Allow fifteen minutes for each individual to study the passage silently and write brief answers to the following questions:

5. What are the main ideas of the passage?

6. What did the stories say to those to whom they were originally addressed? (In answering this question, try to put yourself in the situation of the original audience. Did these words meet a need?)

7. What does this passage say to people today? (What elements are common to the original situation and to our present situation?)

Step 3. For the next twenty minutes go around the circle and share your answers one at a time. Take time to comment on each other's answers or ask questions of one another. Make sure everyone has his turn to share.

Step 4. Allow 5-10 minutes for individual writing of answers to question 8.

8. What is the meaning of the passage for me, right now?
  (a) What changes in my attitudes or actions are called for by my study of this passage?
  (b) Am I ready to accept this demand now?
  (c) What help do I need?

Step 5. Use the remaining time to share your answers to question 8 with each other. Listen carefully with openness to what is being said.

Step 6. Join hands around the circle and spend a few minutes in prayer (silent or spoken) for one another; ask God to encourage and help each one to fulfill his intentions. Designate one member of the group to close the prayer time.

E. SEARCH THE SCRIPTURES METHOD

Mark a sheet of paper into four parts by folding it. Use one-fourth of the paper for each of the following:

1. Point of the passage
2. Parallel Scriptures
3. Problem
4. Profit

Step 1. Personal study. After reading the passage together, allow twenty minutes to fill in the first three sections.

Point of the passage. Go through the passage verse by verse, writing down a brief summary (one sentence) of each verse or each thought.

Parallel Scriptures. In the second section write down any cross references on the topic that come to mind. Or, if there is something in the passage that especially interests you, you may want to look up cross references given in your Bible.

Problems. Here write down any questions you have, or any thought that you don't understand.

Step 2. Ask one person to share his outline, and invite others to add to it or comment on it. Then ask if anyone has parallel references to share.

Step 3. Ask for problems. It is best to list these on a blackboard. If they can be solved in the group readily, spend some time (5-10 minutes) discussing them. If some questions seem more difficult, assign members to find answers and bring them the next week.

Step 4. Allow five minutes of quiet for individuals to write down the Profit of the Passage.

Profit of the Passage. Write down your thoughts regarding the particular meaning this passage has for you, and what you intend to do about it.

Starting with the person next to the leader, share where possible the fourth section. Follow this sharing time with prayer.

Time division

> Step 1: 20 minutes
> Step 2: 5-10 minutes
> Step 3: 5-10 minutes
> Step 4: 20-30 minutes

Search the Scriptures — Sample

> Study passage: Ephesians 4:25; 5:2; 5:15-20
> Time: 60-75 minutes
> Group size: 5 persons

Step 1. Ask God's Spirit to teach you through His Word and through each other. Read the passage through aloud together, about three verses each.

Ephesians was written by the apostle Paul from prison in Rome. It is believed to have been a circular letter to the young churches. The passage we are studying has to do with interpersonal relationships in both the community and the church.

Step 2. In silence, let each individual fill in the worksheet as he studies the passage, working for about twenty minutes. Fill in sections 1, 2, and 3 only. The directions are given on the sample sheet that follows.

Step 3. Ask one person to share his outline, and let everyone add to it or comment on it, or note different ideas. Then share parallel references and discuss problems. Allow twenty minutes for this section.

Step 4. Allow five minutes for each individual to fill in the Profit of the Passage.

Step 5. For fifteen minutes, share what you have written in the "Profit" section. Encourage one another to be honest and specific, especially in regard to actions to take as a result of this study. Discuss ways in which you can help one another.

Take a couple of minutes at the end of your time together to bow your heads and pray silently for one another on the specific intentions that have been shared. Don't forget to commit your own intention to God.

Search the Scriptures Method

Passage: Ephesians 4:25; 5:2; 5:15-20

1. Point of the Passage (Write a one-sentence summary of each verse or thought.)
4:25 Don't lie to each other, either in word, or by silence, because you're all part of each other.
5:2 Be like Christ — Love each other, even if it costs.
5:15 Live wisely.
5:16 Do all the good you can do every minute because we live in evil times.
5:17 For that reason, don't be foolish. Instead try to discover what God wants you to do.
5:18 Don't get your joy from wine. Instead be filled with the Spirit.
5:19 Read the Scriptures together, and sing together to the Lord.
5:20 Thank God for everything in the name of Jesus.

2. Parallel Scriptures (Write down any parallel verses that come to mind, or if a particular thought interests you, look up related passages from cross references given in your Bible.)
4:25 — Col 3:9

5:2 — 1 John 4:10, 11

5:17 — John 6:27-29

5:18 — Phil. 4:4-7

5:19 — Col. 3:16, 17

3. Problems (Any question you have, or anything you disagree with, or don't understand.)

To whom is Paul referring in 4:25 when he uses the word *neighbor*? Is it my "Christian brother," or is it everyone with whom I have contact?

4. Profit
(What did you learn from the study of this passage? What do you intend to do about it?)

1. Absolute honesty with others costs. It's easy to lie by just keeping quiet, but if I am going to love with a Christlike love, I have to be honest even if it does hurt me.
If I live wisely and am a good steward of my time and opportunities, really doing God's will, then I will have nothing I want to hide. And honesty won't be so painful!

2. I am going to make a conscious effort to be more thankful to God from now on.

F. THE PARAPHRASE METHOD

1. If possible, *before* the group meeting begins (or allow twenty minutes of the meeting time for this), read the selected Scripture portions two or three times reflectively. *Then* paraphrase the portion, verse by verse, putting it in your own words. Keep it simple in content — it is no deep theological study. Think about the meanings of words and phrases that you usually take for granted.

2. Note any cross references that come to mind.

3. Summarize or outline your paraphrase. Either first person (I, me, my, us, we) or third person (he, she, him, her, they, them) should be used. An outline form should be a logical, clear arrangement into units by simple topics or sub-headings.

4. Write your own title that best tells what the subject is.

5. Application: What are *you* personally going to do about it?

(a) A prayer: thanksgiving or petition
(b) A record: diary of blessings from the study
(c) A project: something you are going to do *as a result of the study*

6. Group leaders: nothing more than clock-watching referees and motivators (pushers) are needed. The leader should see to it that each one in the group shares, with no one person allowed to use too much time.

7. The meeting periods are to be evenly divided between:

(a) Writing the paraphrase individually, 15-20 minutes;
(b) Sharing paraphrase and summaries, twenty minutes;
(c) Sharing applications and prayer about these. Conversational prayer, twenty minutes.

Paraphrase Method — Sample

Study passage: Galatians 5:13-15,25,26
Time: 75 minutes
Group size: 5 persons

Step 1. Ask God's Spirit to teach you through the Word and through each other. Have one member of the group read Galatians 5:13-15,25,26 aloud.

Remember that Galatians was written by the apostle Paul to the Christians in Galatia. A certain group called the Judaizers were trying to tell the new Christians that they must become Jews if they were going to be Christians. The implication was that they must obey all the laws and observe all the rites of the Jewish faith, including circumcision. Salvation became "salvation by works" — something to be earned — rather than salvation by grace, which had already been obtained for the believer by Jesus Christ in His death on the cross.

For Paul, salvation by grace meant freedom from the demands of the law as well as freedom from its condemnation. But such freedom carried responsibility as well as privileges. In the verses for our study, Paul proposes an alternative to irresponsible freedom.

Step 2. In silence, let each member of the group fill in a worksheet. Allow twenty minutes for this.

Step 3. Take turns reading your paraphrases aloud, stating your title first. Try to discover *why* group members wrote as they did. How does the paraphrase you wrote relate to your own life? Be honest and open and caring toward one another.

Step 4. Take four or five minutes to look over your application. Do you want to add anything to it? Plan a specific and concrete action in response to what you have studied.

Step 5. Share your applications with one another, and tell the group what specific action you plan as a result of the study. Discuss ways that you can help one another.

Take a couple of minutes at the end of your time together to bow your heads and silently pray for one another.

Paraphrase Method

Passage: Galatians 5:13-15,25,26
Title: Liberated to Serve

Paraphrase

Cross References

13 My invitation in the gospel was to liberty. I am no longer subject to the old sinful nature that lives in me. That bondage is broken. But I must not think that because I am free, I can do as *I* like. I am really freed so that I can show my love to others by serving them.

1 Corinthians 8:9

1 Peter 2:16

Ephesians 5:21

14 All the laws of the Old Testament can be summed up in one: I must love others (care for their welfare, desire the best for them in the same way I love and care for myself).

Leviticus 19:18

15 But if I go around criticizing and overpowering others, I'd better realize that someone else will do the same to me, and make me shrink away to nothing too.

25,26 If I say that the Spirit gives me life, I had better live accordingly. There is no room for "I" in my life now; no room for thinking too highly of myself, or making others discouraged or angry; no room for wanting what others have or wanting to be what others are.

Philippians 2:3

Romans 12:3

Summary or Outline
Called to Freedom

— Its use 1. Not an excuse for sin
       2. Liberty to love and serve

— The law 1. Love your neighbor as yourself

Walking in the Spirit
— No self-deceit
— No provoking others
— No envy of others

Application

1. Thanksgiving: that I am not bound to reactions, but free to act positively. I don't have to give in to selfishness and resentments and the power they used to hold in my life, because Christ has made me free.

2. V. 15 Criticism is destructive, not only of the one I criticize, but also of the one who does the criticizing! I criticize my children too much. This week I am going to really work on changing that.

3. V. 26 I drive myself too hard and that is a kind of self-conceit. It "provokes" my family when I get difficult to live with, and it stems from thinking I should be as capable or more capable than others.

COMPARATIVE CHART OF METHODS

Method	Types of Biblical Literature	Strengths	Potential Difficulties	Size of Group
INTERVIEW	Gospel stories of encounters with Christ Examples — Mark 10:17-31 John 9:1-41 Matthew 14:22-33	(1) Fun, helps a group relax (2) Allows participants freedom to "try out" different attitudes to Christ than those already held (3) Easily adapted for different sizes of groups	(1) Limited to use with one kind of Scripture passage (2) Difficult to control time.	4-10 Depends on passage chosen.
SWEDISH	Almost any type of biblical literature Useful for lengthy passages, e.g., Genesis 1-3 Psalm 139 Romans 12	(1) Excellent for use with a group inexperienced in Bible study (2) Variety of biblical literature with which it can be used	Difficult to control time	4-6

Method	Types of Biblical Literature	Strengths	Potential Difficulties	Size of Group
HEAD, HEART, AND HAND (This method usually becomes a favorite)	Most types of biblical literature, especially discourses of Jesus, epistles, teaching passages Recommend passages that naturally fall into paragraphs, e.g., Luke 4:1-15 Colossians 3:1-17 Luke 15:11-32 Eph. 5:21-6:4	(1) Encourages diligent Bible study (2) Easy transition from theory to practical application for individuals as well as the group	Requires more disciplined study so it is sometimes discouraging to beginners who are not accustomed to that	4-6
EIGHT QUESTIONS	Narrative — Old or New Testament New Testament teaching that has its roots in Old Testament Jewish religion and law, e.g., Genesis 12:1-3 Isaiah 42:1-4 Hebrews 10:11-25	(1) Easily used with inexperienced groups because of concise nature of questions (2) Natural transition to practical application (3) Useful for private personal Bible study	Leader must be careful that sufficient time is kept for dealing with the last question	4-6

Method	Types of Biblical Literature	Strengths	Potential Difficulties	Size of Group
PARAPHRASE	Short passage — usually no more than five verses Epistles, teachings of Jesus, Psalms, Old Testament teaching or devotional writing, e.g., 1 Corinthians 13:4-10 1 John 1:5-10 Psalm 1	(1) Strong emphasis on practical application (2) Encourages participants to read Scriptures with a greater awareness of the variety of meaning in words	Some people are more naturally adept at this than others. If this method is used to the exclusion of other methods, some members may become discouraged.	4-6
SEARCH THE SCRIPTURES (similar to Paraphrase)	Epistles, teachings, devotional May use slightly longer passages than with Paraphrase Method, e.g., John 15:1-11 James 5:13-20 Isaiah 11:1-9	(1) Easily learned method (2) Encourages comparison with other passages which result in good doctrinal understanding (3) Useful for individual Bible study.	Requires a little more discipline to make transition to practical application	4-6

6

Prayer as Part of Small-Group Bible Study

Two forms of prayer are invaluable to the life of the small group that has committed itself to Bible study. The first is prayer as a part of the daily life of each individual member of the group, and the second is prayer as part of the actual meeting together.

This chapter will not be concerned with a theology of prayer, nor will it seek to convince you that "prayer works." You will have to discover your own theology of prayer, and by experiment and experience prove its value. (What an exciting time awaits you!) Rather, my purpose is to help you to see how prayer relates to the life of the group and to give some suggestions about how to pray by yourself and with the others.

What Is Prayer?

Prayer might be defined simply as communicating with God. Notice that I did not say "talking to God." "Talking" implies a one-sided effort; prayer involves both talking and listening. At times in our praying there must be silence. I believe there are four basic prerequisites for communicating with God that are relevant to this particular discussion of

81

prayer. The first two have to do with "talking" and "listening."

1. There must be in us a willingness and *a desire to share our lives with God.* We have to want to tell Him what we think and how we feel. That is always the first step in any conversation. There must be a recognition of the presence of the other person which is communicated. That recognition may or may not be verbal. Usually we say, "Hello." In Taiwan, the customary greeting is, "Have you eaten yet?" or "Where are you going?" or perhaps just "Peace!"

Whatever we say or do to indicate that we recognize the presence of the other person, we are communicating a willingness to share ourselves with them. Now, that does not mean that the level of sharing will always be a deep one. Just saying "Good morning" to your neighbor across the fence does not mean that you intend to sit down and pour out your heart to him! You may not plan to tell him anything about yourself; but your recognition of him is a beginning in the relationship.

So it is with prayer. When we begin to pray, we may have reservations about what we want to tell God, but telling Him anything is a beginning to our relationship with Him. As we get to know Him and trust Him, we will share more and more of ourselves with Him.

Sometimes we will verbalize what we want to tell Him. I find it helpful to speak my prayers, not merely think them, when I pray alone. Somehow, it makes prayer more intentional for me. Other times, we just "think Godward." Whatever way we do it, we are indicating a desire to share something of ourselves with God.

2. Another prerequisite for praying is *a willingness to listen to what God wants to share with us.* That means that at times in our praying there will be silence. For most of us, this is the hardest part of praying. There are so many things we want to tell or ask the Lord, but it is so hard to listen to what He wants to tell us.

We are accustomed in our day to loud noises and very explicit messages. The radio and TV blare at us, and life in general is so noisy. We are fast losing our capacity to listen to the "still small voice" whether it be God's or someone else's. But since it is not what we say to God, but rather what He says to us, that changes our lives, we had better learn to listen!

3. There is also *the acceptance of ourselves as we are — sinners*. This *does not* mean that we are constantly to run ourselves down before God. It does mean we are to have no illusions about ourselves when we come before Him. He is holy and we are not. If we think we have anything to bring Him, any "bargaining power," we erect a sound barrier that will prevent us from hearing what He wants to say to us.

What does He want to say? He wants to say that He loves us, that He forgives us, that He wants to help us and direct us. But if we do not recognize our need, those words fall on deaf ears and we are forced to struggle through on our own power.

4. Last is *the recognition of God's absolute and complete love for us just as we are*. God has no illusions about us, even though we may have them about ourselves. He knows our weaknesses, but that does not change His love for us. So we may come to Him honestly — not having to make excuses for our behavior, not having to hide certain aspects of our personality, not having to "put on a good front" — but just as we are, because He *really* loves us. It is our acceptance of ourselves and of His love for us that makes it possible for us to change, to grow — to be re-created in the image of God.

Basically that is what Christianity is all about. God created man in His own image. Man cut himself off from God by disobedience and self-will, and so defaced the image. But God's love reached beyond man's disobedience. He sent His own Son to take upon Himself the burden of our separation and sin, so that we can be re-created again in the image of God. Once we have accepted Christ's death as our death, and begin to seek His life to be our life, the focal point of all our living is to be centered in this one goal: that we should be like Christ.

How brightly the image of Christ shines through our lives is a good measure of how successful we are in our praying. If this sounds pious to you, I suggest that you read through one of the Gospels in a modern version of the Scripture. Read it in one sitting, and as you form a picture of the God-man in your mind, as you catch a glimpse of His values, as you see Him tenderly minister to the needs of the sons of men, ask God to show you how your life would be changed if His image was obvious in you.

Whether prayer is a new experience for us, or an old one, these are four prerequisites for successfully communicating with God —

    1. A will and desire to share our lives with God;
    2. A will and desire to hear what God would say to us;
    3. An acceptance of ourselves as sinners;
    4. A recognition of God's absolute and complete love for us.

A. OUR INDIVIDUAL DEVOTIONAL LIFE

The quality of life in Bible study groups is greatly affected by the kind of devotional life practiced by the group members. That is why the discipline introduced on page 43 calls for at least twenty minutes daily to be spent in prayer and Bible study. In our daily lives we know that building and maintaining a deep relationship with another person, whether it be a friendship, a marriage, or a parent-child relationship, requires a great deal of time and contact. But somehow we think that a deep relationship with God is something that can be "caught," like the measles. Christian joy may be contagious, but spiritual growth is not! We do not build a deep relationship with God simply by being with other Christians; we build it by being with God. We need a constant consciousness of His presence that is firmly founded on regular personal Bible study and prayer.

When each participant in the Bible study group comes to the time of study with open lines of communication between him and God, the lines between participants are open, too. God's love flows along those lines, making the group receptive to the Spirit in their midst, filling them with love for one another, and empowering them as individuals and as a group to be channels of love and blessing to the world around them.

I am convinced that there is never an end to learning in the matter of personal devotions. Maintaining a "quiet time" (as many of us have learned to call it) has been one of the great challenges of my Christian experience — and most of the saints would also testify to that! The temptation to "skip it" or "skim it" is always present. There are frequent growing pains as the Spirit gets down into the dis-ease of our lives. There is anguish and sorrow as God shows us who we are in the mirror of His love and holiness. And there is heartbreak that comes from Christly concern for others.

On the other hand, there are constant rewards of new truth revealed, a deepening sense of the Lord's reality and love for us, new experiences of His presence, moments of ecstasy and joy in worship, satisfaction in being co-workers with Christ when our prayers for others are answered, and the incredible wonder of realizing that Jesus makes us His personal concern.

Because our devotional life is an eternal adventure in learning, I dare to share with you some of the practical tips that have been helpful to me and other adventurers.

First of all, set a regular time and place for your devotions. It will be easier to form and maintain a habit of having a quiet time if you always have it at the same time of the day. Choose a time that is most likely to be free from interruptions. Early morning remains the choice time for most Christians. A surgeon friend remarked to me, "If I don't get my quiet time with the Lord early in the morning, I just don't get it!" Many mothers of young children make the hour after the children have left for school their quiet time; mothers of preschoolers choose nap time. Having it in the morning provides an opportunity to think through the day with the Lord, seeking His will and guidance for every part of it. But there is no hard-and-fast rule. Find a time that is best for you, and stick to it — even when you don't feel like it.

The discipline previously mentioned calls for at least twenty minutes to be spent in prayer and Bible study. Many find, before very long, that this isn't long enough, but it is a good beginning. It is more profitable to spend twenty minutes being really "present" to God than an hour going through a ritual.

Choose a relatively private place, away from the distractions of everyday living. For example, don't sit down at the table among the dirty breakfast dishes after the family has left for the day. And unless you're an extremely disciplined person, don't choose to sit up in bed for your quiet time.

Having found a place and set a time to meet with God, how do we go about it? Keeping in mind the four attitudes described earlier, we may describe the quiet time as a time of communicating with God. We speak to God, and He speaks to us. We speak to Him in prayer, and He speaks to us through His Word and in the silence of our own beings. So basically our quiet times are spent in these two activities: speaking and listening.

Sit in a comfortable chair, body straight, feet on the floor. Close your eyes, take a couple of deep breaths, and relax your body. Open your mind to the Spirit of God, acknowledge His presence. Try to put everything else out of your mind as you prepare to pray.

Elements of Prayer

There are five commonly accepted elements in prayer: praise or adoration, thanksgiving, confession, supplication, and intercession. Praise and adoration consist of contemplating God and pouring out our admiration and love for Him. Many examples of this element of prayer can be found in the Psalms. If this does not come naturally to you (and to most of us it doesn't) use the words of the psalmist to express your own appreciation of God.

Another helpful exercise in praise is to choose one of God's many names and think about all its implications. An example is

"Almighty." Let your mind go as you consider all that it means that God is the Almighty: it means that nothing is too hard for Him; His power is over all the universe, runs the universe; there is no problem that He cannot solve, no circumstance He cannot change, no situation into which He cannot enter, no part of your life that is outside His control. Just revel and wonder at all that, and see how it applies in your own life.

The main reason for praising God and expressing our adoration and appreciation of Him is that He is worthy of far more than all our praise. But praise is also a faith-builder. When we begin to comprehend the wonder of the Godhead, the pieces of our own lives begin to fall into place. The trust factor in our relationship with Him builds up, and we want to share more and more of ourselves with Him. We are ready to put more and more of our lives under His control.

Two elements of prayer are prompted by praise and adoration. Sometimes the thing we feel the most is *gratitude*. When this happens, we move very naturally into thanking God for all He means to us and does for us. Paul tells us we are to give thanks in every situation (Ephesians 5:20; Philippians 4:6; Colossians 3:15-17).

The other possible response to seeing the Lord "high and lifted up" — as Isaiah 6 has it — is an overwhelming sense of our own sin. So we move into the element of prayer called *confession*, or penitence. We confess to God those failures and shortcomings in our lives which He has revealed to us as offenses to Him. We ask His forgiveness through Christ Jesus, and then we thank Him that we have not only His forgiveness, but the assurance that He will cleanse us from our sin and re-create us in His own image (1 John 1:9; 2 Corinthians 3:18).

Whichever of these two responses the Spirit calls forth in us, we must not forget to include the other in our prayers. If we feel called to repentance, we must remember to thank God during our time of prayer. If we sense a rising tide of gratitude within our hearts, let us express it, but then let us learn to wait quietly before our heavenly Father as we ask Him to reveal to us those aspects of our lives that need His cleansing.

The fourth element of prayer is called *supplication*, i.e., asking for what we need. God is our loving, heavenly Father; every need of ours is a concern of His. Paul's experience of the Father's kindness led him to advise the Christians at Philippi to "have no anxiety about anything, but in everything by prayer and supplication with thanksgiving let your requests be made known to God" (Philippians 4:6). Somewhere I read the story of the little girl on her way upstairs to bed whose mother called after her, "Don't forget to say your prayers!" To which the little girl replied, "I won't. Anybody need anything?" Jesus promised, "If you abide in me, and my words abide in you, ask whatever you will, and it shall be done for you" (John 15:7).

The fifth element of prayer to be considered here is closely related to the fourth. *Intercession* is simply asking God to meet the needs of others. Whenever our Lord pours His love and His Spirit into our lives, we may not, indeed we cannot, keep the benefits for ourselves. It always flows over in concern and love for others. As Christians we have not only the privilege, but also the responsibility, of bearing one another's burdens and thus fulfilling the law of Christ (Galatians 6:2).

Intercessory prayer is not an easy ministry, but it is very much needed among God's people. You will want to pray for those closest to you: your parents, sisters, brothers, husband or wife, your children, your friends. Don't forget to pray for your minister and the various leaders of your church. Pray for the leaders in your community and your nation and those on the international scene.

A prayer list often helps greatly in maintaining a consistent work of intercession. Write down the names of those you pray for; some note that reminds you of specific requests you will make on behalf of each one; the date you began praying that request; and a space to write in the date that you became aware of God's answer to that request being evident. Make a habit of checking through the list periodically to see where requests are answered and ask God which may be continued or changed.

You may find that your list grows too long to pray through daily. In that case, ask God to help you sort it out. Decide which persons you should pray for daily, and then divide the other names into several groups. Perhaps you will be able to pray for some of the people on your list only once or twice a week. Whatever you do, pray specific prayers, and don't forget to keep note of answers. This exercise will not only build your faith, but make you an effective intercessor, a co-worker with Christ as He builds His kingdom in our world.

Personal Bible Study

The other part of a quiet time is Bible study, another form of listening to God. Just as our bodies need varieties of food, so do our spirits. It is important that we get a well-balanced diet of Scripture, and that calls for a systematic approach to reading the Bible. If we do not have some kind of plan for reading it, we tend to jump here and there, or get frustrated by our own lack of direction and drop it altogether.

Most denominational headquarters publish some sort of daily Bible reading guide. Others may be obtained at a Christian bookstore. The bibliography in the back of this book gives several suggestions.

You will want to make other time for reading long portions of Scripture at one sitting, but it is probably better to confine yourself to portions of five to fifteen verses (or the narrative of one incident) during your devotional time. If you have allowed a longer period of time (up to forty-five minutes or an hour), you can easily use some of the methods from chapter 3. The Head, Heart, and Hand, the Search the Scriptures, the Eight Questions, and the Paraphrase methods are all useful for individual study. Or you may use these basic questions:

— What does the passage say to those for whom it was originally written?

— What does the passage say to me, in my circumstances today?

— What am I going to do about it?
— What help do I need?

Always remember that the Holy Spirit is your teacher, and you need to ask His help in your study. Keep a notebook in which you record the results of your study. Writing down what God is saying to you will help you to remember His teaching. At times, when you are tempted to think that God never speaks to you, you will find the record of your relationship with Him, and His dealings with you, to be a very real inspiration and help.

There is no "rule" concerning which of these two activities comes first in your quiet time. Sometimes you will want to pray first. Other times it will seem natural to study first.

B. PRAYER IN THE GROUP STUDY PERIOD

One of the most rewarding aspects of this Bible-study program for a large number of participants has been learning to pray aloud with other Christians. Somehow praying aloud is an activity we tend to relegate to the clergy. Those laypeople who dare to pray aloud in the presence of others, we label as either "very devout Christians" or as having "leadership ability." Most of us, unless we have been reared in our homes or churches to do so, are scared to death to pray out loud. The very thought of it makes our hearts stop and our minds go blank.

I recall conducting a workshop in Bible study once, following which one of the pastors told me about his group's experience. We had not intimated prior to the meeting that we would be learning to pray aloud, for the simple reason that one of the planners was sure no one would attend if we did!

When I announced we were going to introduce a method of group prayer, one lady in my pastor-friend's group announced that nobody — but nobody! — was going to get her to pray aloud. Two others vehemently agreed. My friend was afraid they were going to leave, so strongly did they feel about it all! However, as they were gradually brought into the experience in a large group of about forty-five people, I invited anyone in the group who would like to say "thank you" to God, for just anything, to do so. The pastor couldn't believe his ears when the first person to pray aloud was the lady who had so vigorously expressed her intention *not* to pray aloud! And before the prayer time ended, all three had entered joyously into the time of thanksgiving.

Why We Are Afraid

There are many reasons why we are afraid to pray aloud. I believe one is that we think praying requires a special vocabulary. We think we have to know special word forms for addressing God, and that we must know how to get our tongues around all the Thees and Thous. And that makes praying publicly the task of a specialist — namely, the minister.

Another reason why we shy away from praying aloud is that it demands honesty on our part. We know we cannot tell God half-truths. We know He sees behind our masks. Often we do not trust others enough to let them see behind — we may be hurt if we do. Or we are afraid that others will accuse us of a "holier than thou" attitude if we pray aloud.

In small-group Bible study we use a method called "conversational prayer." It has been introduced widely by Rosalind Rinker in her several books on the subject. For that reason, introducing it here would not only be superfluous, but inadequate. I recommend that her book *Communicating Love Through Prayer*[1] be used in conjunction with this one.

Conversational prayer does away with the foregoing reasons for fear about praying aloud. We use ordinary language. God is our heavenly Father: He loves us and does not want something as unimportant as word forms to separate us or to keep us from enjoying all the riches of this meaningful form of Christian fellowship.

The nature of the group itself should relieve any anxiety about the trustworthiness of its members. As you grow in your knowledge of one another through your study and sharing together, you will become more trusting and more worthy of one another's trust.

Prayer will become your deepest level of sharing with one another as well as with God. Your love for each other will expand, and your support of one another will be stronger and more consistent.

The fear of being called "holier than thou" in attitude will be eliminated in short order by the honest expression of needs, confession of sin, and sharing of mutual concern.

Why Pray Aloud?

There are three basic reasons why we encourage prayer as a part of small-group Bible study.

1. Praying about what God has revealed to us in our study of His word is a *seal of our intention* to be obedient to that revelation. When we pray, we are committing ourselves to God's purposes for us. When we pray aloud in the presence of others, we are committing ourselves to God's purposes *before witnesses*. Those witnesses, by virtue of their relationship to Jesus Christ, care about us; they too are committing themselves to God's purposes for us. Therefore we do not take our praying lightly. We intend to do what God has shown us we should do, to the extent that we verbally express it to God in the presence of others. They will be lovingly attentive to how we carry through on what we have said.

2. Another reason for praying aloud is so that we may *experience acceptance*. Until we have expressed our thoughts and ideas, our doubts and fears, our real feelings, we are never completely sure that other people will accept us as we are. Consequently we hesitate to reveal ourselves in case we discover that they do not like us. We may say that we don't care what others think of us, but the fact that we trust ourselves to so few others denies what we say.

It *is* possible that when we do admit who we really are, that when we drop our mask, someone *won't* like us. And we *may* experience hurt. But interestingly enough, we have found it happens rarely during Bible study, and I have never seen it happen during a prayer time. Why? Because we all have to drop our masks when we consciously stand in God's presence. We know that when we see ourselves as we really are, we have no right to criticize or condemn another.

At the beginning of this chapter, four prerequisites for praying are listed. The third is that we accept ourselves as we are: sinners; the fourth is that we remember that God loves and accepts us just as we are. There are two more prerequisites for praying in groups that are closely related: that we accept others as they are, and that we remember that God loves and accepts others of the group in the same way.

Something happens inside us when we pray together. We find ourselves understanding each other and positively reaching out to one another to give support and love in a way that we have never done before. How many times I have heard people say after praying together, "Oh, I'd just like to give everyone a big hug!" (Sometimes we even get outside of ourselves sufficiently to do it!)

All of us need to experience this acceptance because it frees us from the fear of self-concern that so often keeps us from actively expressing our love and caring for others. When we are loved, we are free to love.

3. But probably the strongest reason for including prayer as part of the study period is that by praying, *we actively enlist God's power in our lives*. We admit that we cannot live them out by ourselves — we need help. Asking God for help is a faith-response to His Word. Jesus Himself intimates that there is value in *corporate* asking. In Matthew 18:19,20 He says, "Again I say to you, if two of you agree on earth about anything they ask, it will be done for them by my Father in heaven. For where two or three are gathered in my name, there am I in the midst of them." The key seems to be that Jesus is especially present in a group. Jesus is the Father's obedient Son, and God always hears His requests. When Jesus is in our midst, when

we are truly wanting His will to be done, and when we are openly agreeing together on that, God hears our prayers and answers them.

This is not a "plan of action" that Christians have invented: this is God's plan. He wants us to know this deep level of sharing with Him in the midst of His family; when we are obedient to His desires for us, He honors us for it. We can count on His almighty help in this business of living out our daily lives as salt and light (Matthew 5:13-15) in His world.

How We Pray Together

So . . . how do we pray together? Simply stated, we carry on a conversation with God as a group. We use ordinary language and short sentences. We listen to one another, hearing what is meant as well as what is said, and we try to understand what is being felt. We pray by subjects, and we don't change the subject until we sense that the whole group is ready to do so. Rosalind Rinker describes four steps in conversational prayer in her book *Communicating Love Through Prayer*, mentioned earlier. They are as follows (parentheses mine):

1. Jesus is here (recognizing His presence, welcoming Him);
2. Thank you, Lord (expressing our gratitude);
3. Help me, Lord (telling Him what we need, asking for His help);
4. Help my brother (praying on behalf of others).[2]

I have used these steps as a basis for a series of four Bible studies in chapter 8. If praying aloud together is a new experience for your group, use them as the content of your meetings for a month. Obtain a copy of *Communicating Love Through Prayer* (available at most Christian bookstores) and pass it around among your members. *Conversational Prayer* and *Prayer: Conversing With God* by the same author are excellent helps.[3]

Try to get into the habit of praying together as early as possible in your experience as a group. In one couples' group I know, no one was accustomed to praying aloud with other Christians (unless a spouse). After meeting together three or four times, someone advised the group that vocal prayer was encouraged as part of the Bible study. One lady volunteered to read the printed directions they had been given and to instruct the group. All agreed, and the next week they "tried it out." There were no trained churchworkers in the group: it consisted of businessmen, a carpenter, a teacher, and homemakers. Ordinary, everyday, special people.

Since then, God has literally turned lives upside down in that group. They have discovered that God is very personal in the way He answers prayer. They have discovered that the more specific their prayers, the more specific His answers. All of them testify to a new sense of the Spirit's presence and power in their lives.

Prayer and Bible study in small groups will change your life, too. And as it changes you and upbuilds you as an individual, the church will be changed and upbuilt. For "you are a chosen race, a royal priesthood, a holy nation, God's own people, that you may declare the wonderful deeds of him who called you out of darkness into his marvelous light" (1 Peter 2:9).

7

How To Start a Small-Group Bible Study

Anyone can start a small-group Bible study. It doesn't require an expert. However, it does require a real desire to study the Bible and a real desire to put into action what is learned from that study. If you have these desires, the following steps will help you.

Step 1. Find a nucleus. Talk to your friends and acquaintances, perhaps from your church or in your own neighborhood. Find out if there are others who feel as you do and would like to be part of a Bible study group. Share this book with them and then invite them to your home or some other suitable place to discuss the idea.

Our homes are a part of ourselves that we need to learn to share with others. Peter tells us in his instructions to Christians in 1 Peter 4:8-11 that we are to love one another, practice hospitality ungrudgingly — i.e., share our homes with one another — and remember that all that we have is a gift from God, to be used to glorify the Lord Jesus. Wherever you decide to meet for this first meeting, try to be as free from interruptions as possible.

Step 2. Make specific plans together. It is important that each member of the group have the same understanding of the purpose and process of the group as each other member. The purpose of your first meeting should be to discuss the following elements of group life. These can be applied to any kind of group life, but since we are talking about a specific program, the decisions are basically already made for many of them.

Purpose.   In chapter 1 we stated the goals of this program. Spend a little time discussing these three goals so that all the group understands and agrees to them. They are —

> — To discover what the Word of God is for us today, through the study of the Scriptures;
> — To provide for the nurture and spiritual growth of the group members so that they may be enabled to share the gospel in word and deed;
> — To foster an awareness and understanding of Christian community.

The Size and Composition of the Group

The participants should be fully aware and in agreement as to the size and composition of the group. Too large a group loses its capacity for trust and intimacy; too small a group lacks strength and tends to become undisciplined. Experts in the field of group processes tell us that four is the lowest number and twelve the absolute maximum number for successful relationships in any kind of group. In Bible study groups, we have found four to eight to be most satisfactory.

Composition of the group is important, too. Ideally the group should contain a variety of people, because no matter how different our educational backgrounds, our social standards, our work, or our ages, we can always learn from one another. Earlier it was pointed out that the Christian small group is a lab in which we experiment with "being the church." The church probably has the greatest variety of people in her membership of any organization in the world. A small group experimenting in the reality of being members of the body of Christ can only benefit from variety in the group.

Quite often members will want to invite friends, but it is unwise to add new members until the group has met six or eight times. A trust-relationship between the members takes time to develop. Inviting a new person to participate while the original group is still struggling to build that trust may make the members insecure and defensive. Besides being destructive to the developing sense of community in the group, it may result in a bad experience for the newcomer. A group that is insecure about its interpersonal relationships will not be free to expend its energy and concern on making the new participant feel accepted and welcome.

The Time Factor

Set a time to start the meeting and a time to finish. Once the group has agreed on a time, each member is committed to being punctual. Time is a gift from God, and we are called to be good stewards of it. Some participants in the group may be very busy people: they may not have time to spend a half-hour waiting for other group members to come. Real love for our brothers and sisters in Christ includes respecting time limits. Finishing on time is equally important; those who are free to linger and visit are welcome to do so.

Because this program emphasizes personal growth, we advise meeting weekly. Many people think they are too busy, but again experience has taught us that if the content meets personal needs on a deep level, even the busiest people will make every effort to be on hand.

It is recommended that the first series of weekly meetings consist of eight studies. Most people are more ready to commit themselves to a program if they can see an end to it. Eight weeks provides enough time for the group to develop a sense of community and enough experience of the program to make them want to continue to participate. At the end of eight weeks, members are encouraged to evaluate what has happened to them and make plans for the next series. This is also a good time to invite new members into the group.

Level of Interaction

Bible study groups interact on many different levels, depending on the specific purpose of a group. If a group organizes around an expert in Bible, such as the pastor, and the purpose of the group is simply to hear what he has to say about the Scripture, there will be very little interaction. It will simply be a matter of greeting one another and saying good-by at the end of the lecture. It may or may not include some interaction between the pastor and individuals who ask questions.

A deeper level of interaction may take place in a discussion-type group, but this too will be limited according to the group's purpose. The group may decide, consciously or unconsciously, that they will only interact on an intellectual level. The result here is that individuals may learn a lot of facts about biblical content and theological concepts, but they never help each other to make these facts real in their daily living. Expression of feelings or intimate sharing of personal problems is frowned on at this particular level.

What we are striving for in the kind of Bible study program this book presents is a much deeper level of group interaction. We are looking not just for intellectual growth, but for growth in faith, growth as persons. We seek to promote maturity in Christ. This involves getting down to the feeling level in our lives. It involves sharing the things that really matter to us, the things that hurt, or the things that give us joy and victory. In deciding on a level of interaction, the group will need to recognize that honesty and love are called for. That love is the love of Christ which accepts human beings as they are and gives them freedom to express negative feelings as well as positive. It is the healing, forgiving, and renewing love that enables people to grow up in every way into Christ.

Leadership

This program has shared leadership. Make sure that everyone in the group is aware of this from the beginning.

There are no "experts." This makes it easier for everyone in the group to contribute to the leadership function.

Group Disciplines

On page 43 there is a suggested discipline for group members. Work this over together. Add whatever you feel is important for your particular group and subtract what you feel is unnecessary. Most important are that you pray about it and that each group member makes a definite commitment to the group. Committed participants *grow*. Uncommitted participants make little progress, and they slow down the growth of other group members.

Under this heading, the group may also want to make other, less formal decisions. They include such matters as being honest and open with one another, not repeating to outsiders any personal information that is shared, and determining the role prayer plays in the life of the group. Some decision should be made about refreshments.

Location of the Meeting

It is important that each participant know exactly *where* the meeting will be. The best way to insure that they do know is to have it in the same place each time. If that is not possible, a list should be drawn up giving the dates and location of the meeting that day, with a copy to each group member.

Homes seem to provide a more suitable setting for this kind of meeting, because there is an air of informality and intimacy in a home that is not present in an auditorium or classroom. However, if it is not possible to have the meeting in homes, church halls are next best. Chairs should be arranged in a circle or around a table so that members can all see each other's faces and everyone in the group feels included.

Step 3. Plan the study series. Choose the Scripture passages you wish to study for the first eight weeks. Select the methods of study that are most suitable to the passages chosen. Since the Interview Method is simple and is excellent for helping people relax and enjoy Bible study, it would be a good first choice. Use each method three consecutive times. In an eight-week series you would learn three methods.

Choose a leader for each study. Rotate the leadership week by week so that three different persons have the opportunity to use a method. Help one another as needed. Always remember that you are learning together!

Here are two schedules to help you get started.

Series I — Growth in Christ

Meeting	Leader	Method	Passage
1st week	Mrs. Brown	Interview	Setting Priorities Mark 10:17-31
2nd week	Mr. Black	Interview	Knowing What Happened John 9:1-41
3rd week	Mrs. White	Interview	Stepping Out in Faith Matthew 14:22-33
4th week	Mrs. Green	Swedish	The New Life Ephesians 4:17-32
5th week	Mrs. Brown	Swedish	A Call to Holy Living 1 Peter 1:13-25
6th week	Mr. Brown	Swedish	Keeping It All Together Colossians 3:1-17
7th week	Mr. Black	Paraphrase	Living Out Love 1 Corinthians 13:4-10
8th week	Mrs. White	Paraphrase	The New Life at Home Colossians 3:18-21

At this point, the group would decide whether to continue together as a group and start a new series, or to split into two new groups and invite friends to join them. Whichever the group chooses to do, the next series of eight studies would provide for the teaching of new methods as follows.

Series II — Being the Church

Meeting	Passage	Title	Method
1st week	1 Peter 2:9,10	Who Are We?	Paraphrase
2nd week	Romans 12:1-13	Many Parts — One Body	Head, Heart, and Hand
3rd week	Ephesians 4:1-16	Body Building	Head, Heart, and Hand
4th week	Romans 14:1-15:6	None of Us Lives to Himself	8 Questions
5th week	Ephesians 4:25-5:2	Imitators of God	8 Questions
6th week	James 5:13-20	A Pattern for Fellowship	8 Questions
7th week	Ephesians 6:10-20	The War Is On!	Search the Scriptures
8th week	1 Thessalonians 4:13-5:11	As Those Who Wait for His Coming	Head, Heart, and Hand

8

To Get You Started/46
Bible Studies

The following sutdies are prepared to help you get started in a regular Bible study program using the principles and methods introduced in this book. Each series has four to twelve studies.

The first two series are at the end of chapter 7. They are prepared with a special concern for teaching the group how to use the methods. The content emphasis is on living the Christian life and being God's people.

The subsequent studies do not follow any particular pattern in using the methods, since it is hoped that you will be familiar with all six by this time. Included at the end of this chapter are several Bible studies for Christian festival seasons.

You will find it helpful as you study the Bible to have a variety of translations and paraphrases available to the group. However, I recommend that you use a well known and widely accepted version as a basic study Bible. It is important to differentiate between a *paraphrase* of the Scripture and a *translation*, which seeks to preserve the content of the original manuscripts as completely as is possible.

The Cost of the Christ-Relationship
— Six Studies

Study I — "One thing you lack"

Mark 10:17-31 Rich Young Ruler
Method: Interview (1) the rich young ruler;
                   (2) the disciples.
  or Eight Questions

Study II — Counting the Cost

Luke 14:25-33 "Whoever does not bear his own
    cross . . ."
Method: Search the Scriptures
  or Head, Heart, and Hand
  or Swedish

Study III — "We have only done our duty"

Luke 17:1-10
Method: Head, Heart, and Hand

Study IV — The Ultimate Price

John 12:24-26 (read also vv. 20ff.).
(Note that this discourse follows the triumphal entry
    into Jerusalem and so introduces Jesus' Passion)
Method: Paraphrase

Study V — What's It All For?

Romans 5:1-6 and 8:28-30
Method: Search the Scriptures
  or Head, Heart, and Hand

Study VI — Is It Worth It?

2 Corinthians 4:5-18
Method: Head, Heart, and Hand
  or Search the Scriptures

Ephesians — Twelve Studies
Introduction

This letter was written by the apostle Paul from prison in Rome around A.D. 62. Its style is quite different from the style of his other letters, and this is usually attributed to the fact that he had more time in which to write it. Most of his other letters were written while he was traveling and preaching.

Ephesians is also Paul's most impersonal letter, which seems strange in the light of his having spent three years with the Ephesians. For this and other reasons, it is strongly believed that the Epistle to the Ephesians is, in fact, a circular letter that Paul set down with great care for the purpose of instructing the early Christians in an understanding of the function of the church. The theme of the letter is that all things shall be gathered together in Jesus Christ (Ephesians 1:9,10).

William Barclay describes it thus: "The central thought in Ephesians is the realization of disunity in nature; disunity in man, disunity in time, disunity in eternity, disunity between God and man, and the conviction that all that disunity can only become unity when all men and all powers are united in Christ."[1]

The letter to the Ephesians is very closely connected to the letter to the Colossians. It is believed that Colossians was written first and that Ephesians is an enlargement on the theme of the all-sufficiency of Christ that Paul developed in Colossians. At any rate, Ephesians is considered by many scholars to be the highest and finest of Paul's writings.

In the following outline of studies, questions or suggestions for application and discussion have been included. They should be used as a supplement to the study, and not take the place of discussion that will naturally arise out of the study itself.

Study I — In Christ

Passage: Ephesians 1:1-14
Method: Search the Scriptures
or Head, Heart, and Hand

For application: Write an up-to-date description of a "holy" or "dedicated" person. Share your description with the group. Where do you think you need help to measure up to that standard?

Pray specifically for each member of the group after he has shared his need.

Study II — Vast Resources

Passage: Ephesians 1:15-23
Method: Search the Scriptures
For application: What practical methods have you discovered for keeping yourself conscious of the vast resources in Christ so that you can make use of them in your life?
Share them with your group.

Study III — God's Resources Displayed

Passage: Ephesians 2:1-10
Method: Head, Heart, and Hand
   or Search the Scriptures
For application: What kind of a display of God's resources are you at this point in your life? Why?

Study IV — No More Barriers

Passage: Ephesians 2:11-22
Method: Head, Heart, and Hand
For application: What are some of the barriers erected in our world today that keep men apart from each other and from God? Think about your own community and the barriers that exist there. What can you do about them?

Study V — Paul's Source of Power and Ours

Passage: Ephesians 3:1-21
Method: Swedish
For application: To whom does Paul give the credit for his success as an apostle? Are you able to admit your successes and

give God the glory for them? Does this passage tell you anything about humility? Is there anything you need to do in your life that you've been thinking was impossible? Apply verse 20 to it.

Study VI — The Unity of the Body

Passage: Ephesians 4:1-16
Method: Search the Scriptures
For application: What are the implications of verse 15 (in its context) for your Bible study group? What part of your life needs to be brought under the control of Christ in order that God's church can be built up?

Study VII — Living the New Life/1

Passage: Ephesians 4:17-32
Method: Search the Scriptures
For application: Verse 26 seems to be a plan of action for winning out over anger. Can you think of something in your life that is characteristic of the "old self"? Make a plan for winning out over that characteristic. Don't forget to ask for God's direction and help!

Study VIII — Living the New Life/2

Passage: Ephesians 5:1-20
Method: Swedish
For application: The admonitions of this passage all have to do with relationships. What alternatives does Paul propose to living like "sons of disobedience"? How important is Christian fellowship as a means of enabling us to be imitators of God?

Study IX — Husbands and Wives

Passage: Ephesians 5:21-33
Method: Eight Questions
Notes: In answering question 4 (What historical situation lies behind it?) you will benefit greatly if you do some research on the social conditions of Paul's day as they relate to family life. Again, William Barclay in his commentary *The Letters to the*

Galatians and Ephesians,[2] has an excellent description of the marriage situation and attitudes toward women in New Testament times.

Without some research, you will not begin to grasp the radical nature of Paul's teaching on Christian marriage.

For application: Write a brief description of present-day attitudes toward, and mores in, marriage in your part of the world and in your own community. How radical is Paul's teaching on marriage today? How does your marriage compare?

Study X — Parents and Children

Passage: Ephesians 5:21 and 6:1-4
Method: Paraphrase
For application: What is the "discipline and instruction of the Lord"? What problems do you have in bringing your children up this way?
Share with the rest of the group any practical answers you have found to such problems.

Study XI — Employers and Employees

Passage: Ephesians 5:21 and 6:5-9
Method: Paraphrase
For application: What particular service do you render to society? What is your motivation? What does Paul say should be our motive? How does this affect the quality of your particular service?

Study XII — The Christian's Battle-dress

Passage: Ephesians 6:10-24
Method: Search the Scriptures
For application: Where is the weakest spot in your armor? The strongest? Why? What can you do about the weak spot? Who do you know who needs some strength that your "strong spot" could offer? Make a practical plan for reaching out to that person.

Four Aspects of Prayer — Four Studies

This study does not use one prescribed method. It is prepared particularly for use in groups that are learning to pray together. You will note that each study is correlated with one of the four steps used in conversational prayer as it is described by Rosalind Rinker in her book *Communicating Love Through Prayer*.

Study I — Worship

Step 1. Read Matthew 18:19,20 and Psalm 105:1-7 aloud. Allow ten minutes for silent individual answering of the following questions:

1. What are two implications of these verses for group prayer?

2. Psalm 105:1-7 contains a number of suggestions of ways that we can worship God. Make a list of these elements of worship.

Step 2. Allow 5-10 minutes. Share your findings with one another.

Step 3. Take ten minutes to have one person read the following psalms aloud while the rest of the group notes which of the above "elements of worship" are carried through by the psalmist as he praises God: Psalms 103;111;33.

Step 4. Allow 15-20 minutes. Ask each member of the group to write a short "Psalm of Worship" in his own words, incorporating some of the elements of worship you discovered in Psalm 105. Here is an example, if you need one:

"Thank you, Lord, for your constant presence in my life. This morning you helped me when I had an important decision to make. You have guided my life in so many ways, and kept me safe from harm. You have delivered me from my fear of being alone, and you assure me of your constant care over those I love. You are all-wise and all-knowing, and I am so happy that I know you."

Step 5. Allow 10-15 minutes. For practical application: Ask the members of the group to stand up and join hands in a circle. Bow your heads and close your eyes. Let the leader repeat Matthew 18:20 aloud: "For where two or three are gathered in my name, there am I in the midst of them." Then say, "Thank you, Jesus, for being right here with us."

Allow a moment of silence to recognize His presence. Then one by one, quietly read your Psalm of Worship aloud, starting with the leader. When everyone has read their psalm, the leader will say, "Amen." Close by singing a hymn or chorus of praise that you all know (e.g., the Doxology).

Study II — Gratitude

Thankfulness must always be an integral part of our lives, our personal prayers, and also the prayers we offer as a group — a part of the Body of Christ.

Step 1. Allow twenty minutes. Read aloud Colossians 3:15-17; 1 Thessalonians 5:16-18; and Philippians 4:4-7. Then in silence think about these Scriptures until the twenty-minute time limit has expired.

(a) Make brief notes of the central thoughts.

(b) What particular phrase or thought "gets to you" the most? Put an arrow ⟶ beside it.

(c) Make a list of the ways these passages suggest we should express our gratitude to God.

Step 2. Allow twenty minutes.

(a) Share your notes.

(b) Tell the group where you put your arrow and why that particular thing bothers you. Take time to talk about these problems.

(c) Compare your lists with others' so that everyone has a complete list.

Step 3. Allow five minutes. Make a list of as many things as you can think of for which you should thank God. Remember that 1 Thessalonians 5:18 says to give thanks in all circumstances.

Step 4. Stand in a circle as you did last week, and join hands. Let the leader take you through the first step in conversational prayer by acknowledging the presence of Jesus. Be sure to allow time to worship Him in silence — or aloud, if members of the group wish to do so.

Remember the elements of worship you learned last week. Thanksgiving is one of them. Spend some time now giving thanks to God for the circumstances in your lives and the blessings He has poured out on you. Thank Him for one thing at a time, take turns, and keep your sentences short.

It is not necessary to "close" each prayer. Just say "Thank you, Jesus, for my friend" or whatever you want to thank Him for. When it seems that no one in the group wants to say anything more, the leader should close the prayer.

Try to restrict yourselves to prayers of thanksgiving today. If you have really gotten into the spirit of thanksgiving, you will experience a sense of joy and love for each other. Don't be afraid to express it.

Study III — Petition (Asking God for our own needs)

Step 1. Allow fifteen minutes. Read aloud James 5:13-16; John 14:12-14; Matthew 18:19,20; 2 Corinthians 1:8-11. Ask each person in the group to write down a brief summary of the thought of each passage as it relates to asking God for help.

Step 2. Allow thirty minutes. Share your findings. Discuss and answer the following:

(a) Are there any advantages in praying as a group?

(b) What kinds of situations are suggested as warranting the prayer support of other Christians in these passages?

(c) Are there situations or things that we cannot pray for? Remember as well some of the passages we studied last week, e.g., Philippians 4:4-7.

(d) What gives us the freedom to pray honestly in the presence of other Christians about our own sins and failures? See Ephesians 4:31,32.

Step 3. Allow 5-10 minutes. Write down one problem in your own life that really looms large for you and that you can share with your group. Then write down all the wishes you have that surround that problem. Here are some examples:

Problem	*Wishes*
Relationship with my neighbor	— that the bitterness between us could be healed — that I had the courage to invite her/him over for coffee — that he would agree to a good fence between our yards
My job is not satisfying to me	— that I could find a better job — that I had the courage to quit — that I had more education or training for my job — that my boss would give me more responsibility

Step 4. Allow fifteen minutes. (Leader: Read this section aloud in its entirety to your group first.)

Ask your group to stand and join hands in a circle of love. Acknowledge Jesus' presence in your midst with worship, and spend some time in thanksgiving.

Now, beginning with the leader, take turns telling God and the group about your problem. Express one or two of your wishes in a short sentence — then wait. When one person expresses his problem, let one or all of the other members of the group add a request on his behalf. It might sound like this:

Helen might pray: "Lord Jesus, I have this problem with my neighbors. I know it's partly my fault because my kids ran over his newly seeded lawn. Please forgive me for not watching them more carefully. Please help me to know how to bring healing into our relationship."

George: "Lord, give Helen the courage to go and apologize if that needs to be done."

Amy: "Jesus, please make an opportunity for Helen and her husband [Bill] to be able to talk to their neighbor in a friendly atmosphere."

John: "Help Helen's neighbor to forgive the kids and not hold it against Helen and Bill."

Bill: "Yes, Lord, and please help us to work out a suitable solution to our need for a better fence that will keep the kids and dog at home."

Grace: "Thank you, God, that you are already working in this situation."

When this problem has been prayed through, someone else should share a problem and some of his wishes surrounding it. Continue until everyone has had a chance to pray about a need. Always support one another in any need expressed. This demonstrates your love and concern for the person who shares it.

Study IV — Intercession (Asking God for others' needs)

Step 1. Allow 15-20 minutes. Read the following passages aloud:

> Ephesians 6:18-21
> Ephesians 3:14-19
> Colossians 1:9-12
> 1 John 5:13-18[3]

Then individually study them and list the various requests Paul makes to God on behalf of his Christian brethren. Re-read James 5:13-16 and note the kinds of requests listed there.

Step 2. Allow 15-20 minutes. Share your findings with one another. Is there something particular that stands out for you in what you've read? What is it and why?

Discuss: Are there any situations in which we cannot pray for others? How much do you pray for others? What kind of people should we be praying for?

Step 3. Allow 5-10 minutes. Ask each member of the

group to make a list of three people for whom they might pray, noting a specific need beside each name.

Step 4. Allow 10-15 minutes. For your prayer time today, carry through the period of worship and thanksgiving, omitting prayers of petition for yourselves unless someone has expressed a special need. Pray specifically for each person you have listed. Make specific requests for their needs. Avoid generalizations. Don't forget to thank God for hearing your requests, and for the answers He has already begun to give.

For additional help with intercessory prayer, see Rosalind Rinker's books listed in the bibliography.

Jesus and Human Need in John's Gospel — Eight Studies

Study I — The Need for a New Beginning

Passage: John 3:1-21
Method: Eight Questions
For discussion: All of us at times in our lives experience an aching longing to have another chance, a new beginning. Verses 16 and 17 provide a basis for every new beginning we ever need throughout our lives.

Where do you need a "new beginning" right now? In what way does Jesus give it to you? Share your needs with one another and pray together.

Study II — The Need for Acceptance

Passage: John 4:1-30, 39-42
Method: Interview
Characters to be interviewed include (1) the disciples; (2) the townspeople. (3) the Samaritan woman.

For discussion: Can you recall any time in your life when someone's acceptance of you-as-you-were freed you to be honest about your faults?

Is there anyone in your circle of relationships whom you do not accept as he is — A son or daughter? a husband or wife? daughter-in-law or son-in-law? sister, brother, parent, neighbor, friend? yourself?

Will you share some of the details of the problem with your group and ask them to pray for you as you try to accept that person without asking him to change first?

Study III — The Need for Wholeness

Passage: John 5:1-15
Method: Swedish
For discussion: Jesus is able to make men whole whether the need is spiritual, mental, or physical, but He requires our cooperation. Sometimes, like the cripple in the Scripture passage, we have been lacking for so long that we are used to our own handicap and, deep down inside, we don't really want to change.

Jesus is always asking us to reconsider. Is there a need in your life to which you've become so accustomed that you are just going through the motions of asking for help? Take time to reconsider today. Share your needs with one another and pray for one another.

Study IV — The Need for Bread

Passage: John 6:1-15, 25-59
Method: Eight Questions
For discussion and application: Jesus wants us to know and love Him, not because He has the ability to give us whatever we need, but because He Himself *is* all we need. Once we have our priorities straight, everything falls into place. He does not deny our need for physical bread, but that need is not to be the governing factor in our lives.

What do you think verse 35 means?

What are the priorities in your life? Be honest. Do they need changing? How?

Pray for one another.

Study V — The Need for Freedom

Passage: John 8:31-36; Galatians 5:1,13,14
Method: Head, Heart, and Hand

For discussion and application: The Jews in Jesus' day were under two kinds of bondage: bondage to sin and bondage to the law. Christ was the source of freedom from both kinds of bondage. What kinds of bondage are we under in our day? What kinds of bondage parallel the Jew's bondage to the law? Is there some kind of bondage in your life that keeps you from freely responding to God and those around you? Share it with your group if you can, and pray for one another as you claim the Truth to set you free.

Study VI — The Need to Express Our Worship

Passage: John 12:1-13
Method: Interview

Characters to be interviewed are (1) dinner guest, (2) Judas Iscariot, and (3) Mary.

For discussion: If Jesus were here in our midst in physical form, how would you like to express your feeling toward Him?

How can we express our worship and love for Him, since He is present by His Spirit, whom we cannot see or touch?

Read Matthew 25:40.

Ask the Lord to show you one of His "brethren" through whom you might express your love for Christ. Write out one tangible thing you would like to do for that person for Jesus' sake. Share your intentions with the group, and pray for one another. Don't forget to carry out your intention before next week.

Study VII — The Need for Identity

Passage: John 15:1-17
Method: Search the Scriptures

For discussion: From this passage, find as many factors as you can which give identity to a child of God. Share your needful aspect of identity with your group, and pray for one another as you thank the Lord that He is the source of your identity. What aspect of your own identity are you unsure of: your importance to someone else? the usefulness of your life? the purpose of your life? that you are loved? your "roots"? your future? what else?

Study VIII — The Need for a Savior

Passage: John 19:1-30

Method: Ask one of your group who is an expressive reader to read this passage aloud while the others listen with eyes closed. After the reading, each person will quietly write an imaginary account of the feelings of some person who was present at the Crucifixion that day. Pretend you are that person and you are making an entry in your diary or writing a letter to a very close friend. Think how you would feel.

After twenty minutes, go around the group, each one reading aloud what he has written and sharing your ideas or questions.

For discussion: What does it mean to you that Jesus met your need for a Savior? Why do you need a Savior?

Jesus obviously believed that humanity needed a Savior, someone to take a person's sin and pain upon Himself and bear man's punishment. Do you really believe it? What kind of results should be evident in our lives if we really believe that Jesus' death on the cross was important for us?

During your prayer today, spend some time thanking Christ for His great and willing sacrifice.

God's Person in Today's World — Six Studies

Study I — The Profit of Godliness

Passage: Psalm 1

Method: Paraphrase

For discussion: In the light of the gospel as we find it in the New Testament, how do you define *wicked* and *righteous?*

What profits of godliness do you find expressed in this psalm? How do you see those profits expressed in your own life?

Study II — "Help, Lord! I've got problems"

Passage: Psalm 6
Method: Paraphrase
For discussion: How does the writer of this psalm feel? Do you ever experience those feelings? What is the source of the psalmist's problems? What does he do with the problems?

Do you have a problem in your life that you need to put in God's hands? Have you honestly told God how you feel about the problem and asked Him to deal with those feelings?

Study III — "In the midst of a wicked and perverse generation"

Passage: Psalm 12
Method: Paraphrase
For discussion: Compare this passage with Philippians 2:14-16 and today's newspaper. How do the characteristics of the society of David's day compare with those of Paul's day and of our own time? As Christians, we are called "to shine like stars" in our dark world. Do you need to confess any of these sins and seek the Lord's cleansing today so that you may be counted among those who bring light instead of adding to the darkness?

Study IV — "I'm glad I'm on Your side, Lord"

Passage: Psalm 16
Method: Paraphrase
For discussion: Verse 4 — What are some of the gods that people choose as worthy of their lives today? In what ways do we find ourselves joining in the ritual or getting caught up in the trend to pay them homage? According to the psalmist, what are the results of determinedly choosing the Lord?

Ask the Lord to show you whether verse 8 could truly be your testimony.

Study V — "I know whose world this is!"

Passage: Psalm 24
Method: Head, Heart, and Hand
For discussion: The attitude of the Christian toward the

flow of history should be one of joyous optimism, because he knows whose world this is and he knows that history flows toward the coming of the King of Glory.

Is there any aspect of pessimism in your life today? What happens when you set it beside the word-pictures of verses 1, 2, 7-10?

Study VI — "With Your help, Lord, I'll make it!"

Passage: Psalm 27
Method: Search the Scriptures
For discussion: Unlike David, most of us do not have human enemies who are seeking our death. However, the principles which David introduces as the means by which he lives a victorious life can be applied to other kinds of battle. Read Ephesians 6:12.

What are some of the temptations you face that make it difficult to live the Christ-life? How does this psalm apply to your life?

Share with one another, and pray about these things together.

The Advent Adventure
— Four Studies for the Christmas Season

Study I — The Advent Adventure for Israel

Introduction:
Isaiah was probably the cousin of King Uzziah. His ministry extended over a period of about forty years — 740 to 701 B.C. He was a statesman who, amid the political issues of his day, preached the word of God and sought to interpret His will. He was also God's spokesman through whom God made known to His people His purposes for the present and the future.

The prophecies which we will look at in this study probably had a local and historical significance to Isaiah and the leaders of his time. The coming of Christ poured new meaning into the prophecies, and as Christians we may look back at them with complete understanding.

Passages: Isaiah 2:1-5
           Isaiah 7:14
           Isaiah 9:1-9

Read these passages together and discuss using the questions given below.

1. *Isaiah 2:1-5.* Often, when God gives promises, He gives them in answer to specific longings and needs that His people express.

(a) What kind of needs do you think prompted God to make these promises? What will be the characteristics of this wonderful day? What did Israel long for? Write on a blackboard or paper.

(b) Read 2 Corinthians 6:16b. If the church (the people of God) is the temple or dwelling place of God in our world today, what do you learn of its purpose in the world?

2. *Isaiah 7:14.* Immanuel — "God with us." What kind of longing among His people prompted this promise from God?

3. *Isaiah 9:1-9. (The Living Bible* is useful in this passage.) This prophecy comes as an encouragement to Israel, which is passing through a time of great suffering and darkness. God promises that the darkness will end because He is going to send a great light.

Verses 2-5:

(a) What will be the characteristics of that time? Note briefly.

(b) How does God hope to accomplish this? (v. 6)

(c) Individually list on your paper the names that are given to describe the promised Messiah in verse 6. Opposite each name jot down what you think these titles indicate about the people's longings — e.g., "Wonderful" might suggest that they were looking for a hero, someone to look up to, to respect, someone who would be entirely different from themselves in that He would be a truly worthy person.

Note that the Hebrew word for *peace* is *shalom*, which means not merely a cessation of war, but a condition of prosperous, harmonious, and positive well-being.

After allowing 5-10 minutes to do this quietly, share your ideas with one another and add to your own list. In silence, go through your list and pick out the longings of your own heart.

Can — or does — Jesus satisfy these longings for you? Be honest! Why? *or* Why not?

What special thing do you want Jesus to do for you today?

Can you think of a name for Jesus that would indicate that He can and will supply your longings? Call Him by that name this week.

Study II — The Advent Adventure for Four People

Passages: Matthew 1:18-25
           Luke 1:1-2:24

For six or eight people.

(Leader: Be familiar with the Interview Method found on pages 57,58 before you attempt this study).

Part 1. Allow 15-20 minutes. Have one of the members of the group pray, asking God's Spirit to guide the group into truth and understanding.

Read the passages for study aloud, taking turns around the group with each person reading twenty verses each.

Here is some background information to help you understand the passages.

    (a) Betrothal customs. In the Jewish marriage there were three steps:

        (1) *Engagement.* This agreement was made by the families of the couple concerned and often while the couple were yet children and possibly had never met.

        (2) *Betrothal.* This was the ratification of the engagement. It lasted for a period of one year and was as binding as marriage. The couple were known as man and wife, but they did not yet

have conjugal rights. The betrothal could be broken only by divorce.

(3) *Marriage proper.*

(b) The name *Jesus* is the Greek form of *Joshua*, which means "Jehovah is salvation."

(c) It would seem that Mary and Joseph were extremely poor, since in Luke 2:24 we are told that they took two young pigeons to the temple for her purification rites. Compare Leviticus 12:6-8.

Part 2. Allow fifteen minutes. Divide the group into four teams of two.

Team 1 will be Elizabeth and an interviewer.

Team 2 will be Zechariah and an interviewer.

Team 3 will be Mary and an interviewer.

Team 4 will be Joseph and an interviewer.

An alternative division for a group of six would be two teams of three comprising (1) Elizabeth and Zechariah and one interviewer; (2) Mary and Joseph and one interviewer.

In your teams of two (or three) spend the next fifteen minutes learning all you can about the particular person(s) you have been assigned and what the person(s) experienced and felt about Advent.

Prepare an interview in order to present to the rest of the group what you consider the interesting and important details of your character's experience. Do not spend time on the prophetic utterances of Luke 1:46-55 and 68-79, since the next Advent Adventure is concerned with a deeper study of them.

Part 3. Allow 20 minutes. Give each team five minutes to present its interviews to the rest of the group. After the presentations, discuss together the answers to these questions:

1. What new thing(s) did you learn from the Christmas story?

2. What kind of people were Mary and Joseph, Elizabeth and Zechariah? Do their lives have anything to say to your life today?

Close with prayer.

Study III — The Advent Adventure for the World

Passages: Luke 1:46-55, 68-79

(Leader: You will need scissors, paste, some old magazines, and a piece of heavy card approximately 12 inches x 18 inches for this session.)

Part 1. Allow twenty minutes. Pray that God's Spirit will guide you into truth and understanding as you study.

Read aloud the two passages for study.

Allow fifteen minutes for silent individual study of the passages, with pencil and paper in hand.

Make a list in your own words of the effects Christ is to have on the world (i.e., society). Write down any new thoughts or questions you have about the passage.

Part 2. Allow twenty minutes for sharing your findings with one another.

William Barclay suggests that Christ brings *moral, social,* and *economic* revolution to our world.[3] Can you think of some concrete examples of these revolutions (a) in the world; (b) in your own community; and (c) in your own life? Share these examples with the group.

Part 3. Allow twenty minutes. Using the piece of heavy card as background, cut pictures and slogans from the magazines and make a collage that expresses what it means to society that Jesus Christ came to live in our world and share our lives.

Close with prayer.

Study IV — The Advent Adventure for God

Phase I

1. Read *John 1:1-5, 9-18.* Remembering that Jesus is God's Word, the Logos, what do you learn about His relationship to God in these passages? What two attitudes toward Jesus are held by humankind?

2. Read *John 3:16,17.* What do you learn of God's rela-

tionship to the world through these verses?

3. Read *John 3:35*. What is God's attitude toward Jesus?

4. Read *John 8:25-30* and *Isaiah 53:6*. Write a comparison by considering the following:

(a) God's attitude toward Jesus and His attitude toward mankind;

(b) God's relationship to Jesus and His relationship to mankind;

(c) Jesus' attitude to God and mankind's attitude to God.

Note the tension here. If Jesus were your son, what would you have done at Christmas?

Phase II:

Use the next fifteen minutes to discuss your answers.

Phase III:

Have one person in the group read John 19:1-19 from *The Living Bible*. Luke 23:44 tells us there was darkness over all the earth.

Now read Luke 2:1-20 aloud. Note that the skies were bright with the light — the heavens celebrating, as it were.

What attributes of God were displayed that night?

Read Isaiah 53:10-12 aloud.

Close with worshipful prayer.

Consider Him
— Six Studies for the Lenten Season

"Consider him who endured from sinners such hostility against himself . . . " (Hebrews 12:3).

Study I — "Wounded for our transgressions"

Passage: Isaiah 53

Method: Swedish

For discussion: In the light of all that Jesus suffered for us, how should the Christian deal with the problem of sin in his life? The atonement of Christ is the basis for our living positive, joyful, victorious lives. Is there some sin (failure, habit, relationship) in you that causes you to be discouraged? How can you apply Jesus' atonement to your need today? Don't let Jesus' suffering and death be for nothing in your life!

Study II — The Last Supper

Passage: Luke 22:7-39
Method: Head, Heart, and Hand
For discussion: After studying this passage, select a color that you feel symbolizes the mood of the Last Supper. Then think of a sound that would describe it, and write down two adjectives. Each member should take his turn to tell the group what color, sound, and adjectives he has chosen.

How does Luke's particular description of this last time of fellowship together compare with the picture you usually have in your mind?

Study III — The Loneliness of Gethsemane

Passage: Matthew 26:30-46
Method: Swedish
For discussion: How do you think the disciples felt about this incident? What was Jesus' attitude toward them?

This passage demonstrates Jesus' humanity as few others do. Make a list of the human characteristics to be found in it.

As human beings, we too must choose whether we bring our humanity into obedience to God, or succumb to its weakness.

Study IV — The Betrayals

Passage: Matthew 26:14-16, 47-58, 69-75; 27:1-5
Method: Head, Heart and Hand. (Under the "Head" section, summarize each group of verses. Contrast and compare Peter and Judas in their acts of betrayal.)
For discussion: Note in verse 56 that all the other disciples fled. This, too, is a kind of betrayal. Who of us is without sin? What should we do when the Spirit points out betrayal in our

lives? What are some of the subtle ways that we betray Christ? Other people?

Study V — The Trial and Crucifixion

Passage: Matthew 26:57-68; 27:1-66
Method: Adaptation of the Interview Method
Read the passages aloud together. Assign each member of the group one role. Roles to be played are —

(a) Caiaphas, the high priest
(b) Pilate, the governor
(c) One of the soldiers in the crucifixion detail
(d) Simon of Cyrene
(e) Mary Magdalene (see Luke 8:2,3)

Allow ten minutes for each character to read parallel passages in Mark, Luke, and John. Then the whole group will take turns asking each character (focusing on one character at a time) questions as if at a news conference.

After thirty minutes, let each person individually and silently pick out the idea or fact that stands out most meaningfully for him. Share these thoughts with one another and close your time together with prayer.

Study VI — The Resurrection

Passage: Luke 24:1-52 and John 20 (parallel passages are Matthew 28; Mark 16).
Method: Interview Method as used in Study V. Roles to be played are —

(a) Mary Magdalene
(b) Cleopas
(c) Simon Peter
(d) Thomas

For discussion. Did Jesus' followers *really* expect Him to rise from the dead? What difference did it make to them? What difference does it make to you?

9

Two Leadership Training Programs

A. THE ONE-DAY WORKSHOP

The one-day workshop is designed as a method for rapidly introducing a small-group Bible study program to a large number of people. Ideally these are people with known leadership abilities who are already taking responsibility in their communities and parishes. This workshop is suitable for training leaders in a community or district. It can be denominational or interdenominational, depending on the purposes of those who organize it.

One drawback of the one-day workshop is that it may not be thorough-enough training for the participant who lacks initiative. Sending participants in pairs from a congregation or locality may help to ensure that the material presented is put to good use after the workshop has ended.

Planning for the Workshop

The first prerequisite for planning a good workshop is a good planning committee. Three to five persons who are keenly interested in the project are sufficient. The following are details that will need to be arranged. Be sure that responsibility for each detail is assigned to someone on your committee.

1. Participation

(a) Who will attend? Remember that this plan works best if the participants are definitely leadership material. Former experience in committee work, study or task groups, teaching, etc. will make it easier for the participant to assimilate the information presented during the day.

What geographical area will the workshop serve?

Will the participants come from a distance? If so, do arrangements need to be made for overnight lodging?

Will participation be on a denominational level? community level? What age-groups?

(b) How many people? Any number is possible, depending on the size of the facilities. Fifty is a manageable number.

(c) How will the workshop be publicized? Who will accept registrations? How soon prior to the date of the meeting will registrations be required?

2. Facilities

(a) Decisions required to facilitate the workshop include setting a date and finding a suitable place to have it.

If you plan to serve a wide geographical district, choose a central location. Churches and schools usually provide the best accommodations. You will need one large room with movable chairs. If the room is quite large, you may be able to set it up for the lecture sessions and the small-group sessions simultaneously. In that case, small tables large enough for 4-6 people to sit around comfortably are an asset (see Figure A).

If the room is not that large, set up for the lecture period first, but have a large chart visible showing which groups will meet where in the room during small-group periods. This will save time during the rearrangement interim (see Figure B). I have found it easier to work with a group using this arrangement than with having small groups go to other rooms for the study period. Make sure the room is well lighted and has restrooms nearby.

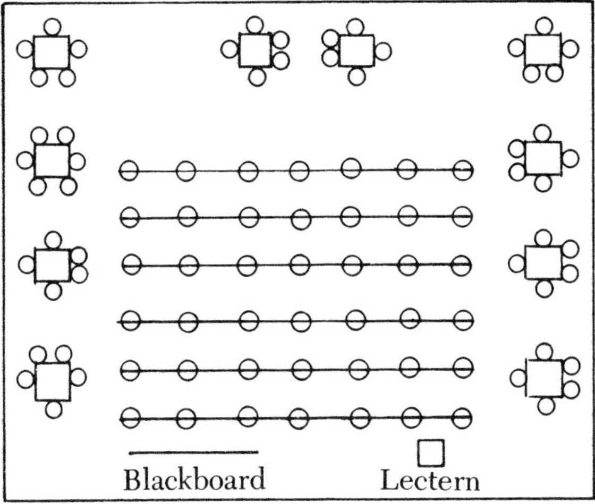

Figure A

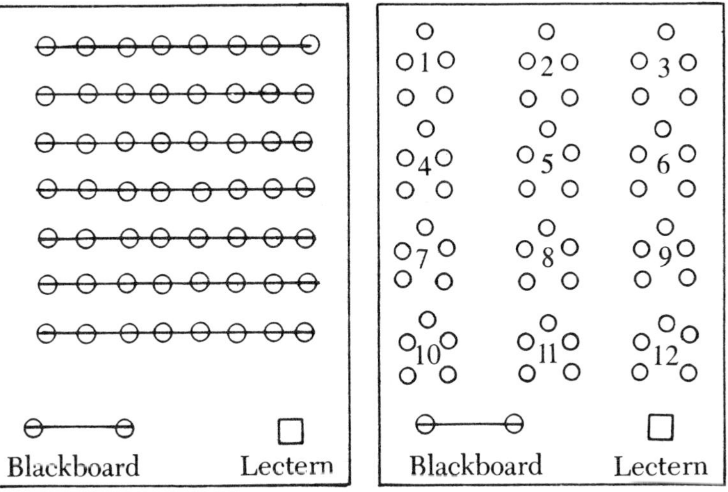

Figure B

Lecture period   Small-group sessions

(b) Hospitality. It will be necessary to provide for a noon meal. Sometimes a women's group in the hosting church will provide a luncheon. Or you may arrange to have lunch sent in from a local restaurant that provides a take-out service; or you can simply ask participants to bring a bag lunch. Beverages should be provided at the workshop.

Coffee and tea available for participants as they arrive is a great help in encouraging a spirit of fellowship, besides being a refreshment to those who may have driven for a few hours prior to arrival. A coffee break is scheduled for midafternoon as well.

(c) Work materials. A chalkboard (with chalk and eraser) and a small table or lectern will be useful to those who give the lectures. An overhead projector is often preferred to a chalkboard when one is available. All participants will need paper and pencil and a name tag.

(d) Finances. Organizations may have different ways of financing a workshop like this, but one simple way to do it is to charge each participant a registration fee that will cover his share of the cost of —

> Securing facilities
> Coffee and noon meal
> Materials used
> Resources, including printed material and personnel
> Miscellaneous

Some cost attached to the workshop gives participants a greater sense of its importance and calls forth a deeper commitment to the experience. For that reason, I suggest that whether or not you subsidize the workshop, each participant should be required to pay a registration fee.

3. Leadership resources

(a) Personnel. The schedule calls for two half-hour lectures and a one-hour session on learning conversational prayer. The purpose of the lectures is simply to introduce the material in chapters 1 and 7 of this book as quickly and efficiently as possible. Choose someone who speaks well to prepare the material. Ideally it should be a person who has had experience in small groups. You may decide to ask one person to do both of these sessions.

Teaching conversational prayer is a very important facet of the workshop. Seek someone who is accustomed to using this method of praying and who has taught it to others. If you cannot find an experienced person, find someone who is capable, sensitive to other people, believes in the power of prayer, and will try to teach it. Well in advance of the workshop give him copies of *Prayer – Conversing with God, Communicating Love Through Prayer, Praying Together,* and *Conversational Prayer,* all by Rosalind Rinker.[1]

Suggest that he practice-teach this method to some small groups of his friends. *Conversational Prayer* has "dry runs" in it, and all the material needed to teach others. Anyone who can summon a little courage, and really wants to teach others to pray can do it if he follows the excellent directions Miss Rinker gives.

One person will need to serve as a *coordinator* for the day's program. He might be asked to conduct the brief worship time scheduled at the beginning of the day, and to lead the evaluation and question period at the end. The coordinator's task is to enable the group to move from one activity to another. He will need to know the plans for breaking up into groups, the arrangement of the chairs, the meal, and coffee breaks. It is important that he know what directions to give to the group and how to give them clearly and succinctly. The tenor of the day is to be informal, but not inefficient.

He will also be responsible for giving a *brief* introduction to each of the Bible study methods to be used. Choose your coordinator carefully. His is a very important task. You may have good lectures, good material, and great participants, but if you have a confused coordinator, people may go home from the workshop feeling insecure instead of enthusiastic and ready to start a Bible study group in their own community.

Coffee breaks and lunch will require some personnel resources too.

(b) Printed materials. Ideally every participant should have a copy of this book. The Bible studies to be used in the workshop are printed here, and that would nullify the need for reprinting them.

More important, though, is the fact that this workshop really gives just a taste of what a small-group Bible study program is all about. This book will provide helpful resources for skills and program long after the workshop is past.

A book display will be appreciated by most people. Try to have a supply on hand to sell; a local Christian bookstore may help you in this. If that is not possible, provide order forms. The bibliography on page 141 will suggest books helpful in starting Bible study groups.

The Workshop Itself

Suggested schedule:

9 - 9:15 A.M. Registration and coffee

Registrar: Give each registrant a name tag with his name and a number on it. Put the same number on each of five name tags. You will know approximately how many people are planning to attend; if you have fifty registrants, you will have ten piles of five name tags numbered from one to ten.

Participants will join with others who have the same number for study groups. Therefore people who come from the same church or community should be given different numbers. Each group of five people should be representative of different localities or congregations. This will ensure greater freedom for the participants in sharing and a broader experience of the workshop for the churches represented.

Each registrant should receive worksheets, a pencil, and a copy of *Bible Study Can Be Exciting!*

9:15 - 9:30 Worship

Worship should include lively music and singing, a brief passage of Scripture, and prayer for the guidance and help of the Holy Spirit during the day. No sermon.

9:30 - 10:00 Introductory lecture

This should be based on the contents of chapter 1 of this book.

10:00 - 11:15 Interview Method of Bible Study

Introduce the method briefly (5 - 10 minutes).

Divide into groups of five according to the numbers on name tags. Rearrange chairs if necessary. Make sure that each group knows where it is to convene.

Have each group appoint an "initiator." The coordinator may suggest that the person whose birthday is closest to the day at hand will be the initiator.

Have everyone turn to page 58 and begin the study of Matthew 14:22-33.

The initiator will read the directions and keep time. The "Bible study leader" for this hour is the printed page.

11:15 - 12 Introducing conversational prayer

Leader: While teaching steps 3 and 4, have participants divide up into their own groups of five.

12 M. - 1 P.M. Lunch break

1 - 2:30 Head, Heart, and Hand Method *or* Eight Questions Method

Use the same plan as for the Interview Method. Introduce the method of choice.

Open the book to page 65 for the Head, Heart, and Hand study of Colossians 3:9-17 *or* to page 69 for Eight Questions study of Matthew 22:1-14.

Encourage the groups to use the last five minutes for conversational prayer.

2:30 - 3 Lecture: "How to Start a Group" (based on chapter 7).

3:00 - 3:15 Coffee break

3:15 - 4:30 Paraphrase Method *or* Search the Scriptures Method

Use the same plan as before.

The Paraphrase study of Galatians 5:13-15,25,26 is found on page 75; the Search the Scriptures study of Ephesians

4:25-5:2 and 5:15-20 is found on page 72.

4:30 - 5:00 Evaluation and question period

On page 47 there is a simplified evaluation check sheet. A mimeographed copy of such a sheet for each participant will help him pinpoint his feelings about the day and help the planning committee in arranging for future events. It can be filled out quickly and passed in unsigned. Use the rest of the period for questions and discussion of the day's content.

OR

3:00 - 4:15 Paraphrase Method/Search the Scriptures Method

4:15 - 5:00 Coffee during evaluation and question period

B. THE EIGHT-WEEK LEADERSHIP TRAINING PROGRAM

The eight-week program is designed for use in a local congregation or community and is geared for a group of eight to twelve people. It requires two hours weekly to be spent in the group session and encourages homework in the form of assigned reading and preparation, as well as supplemental reading as time permits.

This program provides more thorough training than the one-day workshop, since there is more time for learning skills. The actual group experience is more intense and highly instrumental in bringing about the deep commitment to small-group Bible study that usually results from this eight-week program.

It is sometimes difficult to get people to commit themselves for eight consecutive weeks, but it is worth the effort. Once started, most participants will do their very best to attend.

Each meeting calls for a half-hour presentation of some aspect of group life, introduction of the method of Bible study to be used, and 1¼ hours in actual Bible study. Divide your group into smaller groups of 4-6 persons for the Bible study period. It is best to keep the same study groups throughout the course.

In planning for the eight-week program, it is not necessary to set up a formal committee. One person may be the initiator. Usually this is the case when someone (like yourself?) gets enthusiastic about starting some study groups in his community and succeeds in getting others interested in the idea. Together you will look over this program and decide who is going to take responsibility for specific parts of it. Or it may be that someone in the group is experienced and has the time to take responsibility for the whole program.

Whichever way your group does it, draw up your program schedule with each part assigned to someone *before* the course begins. The main resources will be the group members themselves, this book, and the Bible. The Holy Spirit is always your teacher.

A centrally located home or a lounge or small classroom in the church is a possible meeting place. It is best to meet in the same place all eight weeks. Refreshments may be served, but preceding or following the study period, not during it.

Each participant will need a Bible, notebook, pen, and ideally a copy of this book. Resource books for those who want to do supplemental reading are suggested in the bibliography. Check your church or public library or your minister's study also.

Outline of the Eight-Week Program

First Week

(a) "Goals and Principles of Small-Group Bible Study," based on chapter 1 of this book. Allow thirty minutes for lecture and/or discussion.

(b) Introduction to the Interview Method of Bible study found on pages 56-58 (fifteen minutes)

(c) Bible study. Use the sample study of the Interview Method on pages 58-60 (1¼ hours).

(d) Assignment for next week: chapters 2 and 3 and pages 63,64 in *Bible Study Can Be Exciting!*

Second Week

(a) "Responsibilities of the Servant-leader and the Servant-member," based on chapter 3. Allow thirty minutes for lecture and/or discussion.

(b) Introduction to the Head, Heart, and Hand Method found on pages 63,64 (fifteen minutes)

(c) Bible study. Use the sample study of the Head, Heart, and Hand Method on pages 64-67 (1¼ hours).

(d) Assignment for next week: pages 60, 61 and chapter 6, pages 81-90 in this book.

Third Week

(a) "Devotional Life of the Participants," based on chapter 6. Allow thirty minutes for lecture and/or discussion.

(b) Introduction to the Swedish Method (fifteen minutes)

(c) Bible study. Use the sample study of the Swedish Method on pages 61-63 (1¼ hours).

(d) Assignment: pages 67,68 and chapter 6, pages 90-95 in this book. If possible, distribute copies of one of Rosalind Rinker's books on conversational prayer.

Fourth Week

(a) "The First Two Steps of Conversational Prayer," based on chapter 6. The leader for this session and the next should prepare by reading *Communicating Love Through Prayer* (see bibliography). Allow thirty minutes. Include an actual prayer experience.

(b) Introduction of Eight Questions Method found on pages 67, 68 (fifteen minutes).

(c) Bible study. Use the sample study found on pages 68-70 (1¼ hours).

(d) Assignment: pages 71, 72 and chapter 2 in this book

Fifth Week

(a) "Steps Three and Four of Conversational Prayer" (thirty minutes). Include an actual prayer experience.

(b) Introduction of Search the Scriptures Method found on pages 71, 72 (fifteen minutes)

(c) Bible study. Use the sample study found on pages 72, 73 (1¼ hours).

(d) Assignment: chapter 7 and page 74

Sixth Week

(a) "How to Start a Group," based on chapter 7. Lecture and/or discussion

(b) Introduction to the Paraphrase Method (fifteen minutes)

(c) Bible study. Use the sample study of the Paraphrase Method on pages 75, 76 (1¼ hours).

(d) Assignment: review chapter 5 and write down any questions you have about the methods.

Seventh Week

(a) "Comparison of the Methods." This session should include a discussion on how to choose a method for any given passage of Scripture and provide some practical experience. Plan a series of studies of your own, choosing a theme or a short book of the Bible, dividing it up into reasonable portions and choosing a method of study for each portion. See pages 77-79 for a comparative chart of methods. Discuss any questions participants raise about methods during this session (two hours).

(b) Assignment: chapter 4 of this book

Eighth Week

(a) Evaluation of the course and discussion of problems encountered. Those who have been doing extra reading will have helpful materials and insights to contribute at this point. If questions are raised for which you do not, as a group, have satisfactory answers, make plans for getting those answers from other sources (one hour).

(b) "Planning Ahead" exercise (forty-five minutes). Begin this exercise with the whole group together.

Step 1 (ten minutes). Hand out paper and pencils, and ask the participants to write an answer to each of the following:

— Write down the names of three people whom you would like to invite to join a Bible study group.

— What do you want to happen in that group? What do you picture happening to the three people on your list if they attend?

— What part of leading a Bible study group do you most fear? Why?

— What do you conceive of as your "gift" in leading a Bible study group?

Step 2 (thirty minutes). Have the participants get together in their regular study groups, with chairs arranged in a close circle.

Choose one person. Let each member of the group tell that person what he thinks is the gift he brings to a Bible study group. For instance, if Tom is selected to be first, Mary might say, "Tom, I think your great sensitivity to other people's feelings is the gift you bring to a Bible study group," while George might say, "Tom, I think that the way you draw other people out and get them talking is your gift."

After each person has affirmed the first person (e.g., Tom), let him share the answers he wrote down for the questions in the third and fourth parts of step 1.

Move around the group until every one has received the group's affirmation and has had an opportunity to share his answers.

Step 3. Join hands and spend a few minutes in prayer for one another.

(c) Celebrate your experience of the past eight weeks by joining in a circle and singing a hymn together. This is a good day for refreshments.

Notes

CHAPTER TWO

[1] This list is reprinted with permission from *Church Meetings That Matter* by Philip A. Anderson; copyright © 1965 United Church Press. Available from United Church Press, 1505 Race Street, Philadelphia, PA 19102.

CHAPTER FOUR

[1] Origin of these questions is unknown.

[2] From *Learning Together in the Christian Fellowship* by Sara Little. © 1956 by C. D. Deans. Used by permission of John Knox Press.

[3] Clyde H. Reid, *Groups Alive – Church Alive* (New York: Harper & Row, Publishers, 1969), p. 60. Used by permission.

CHAPTER FIVE

[1] See bibliography for suggestions.

[2] Lyman Coleman, *RAP a Minicourse in Christian Life Style* (Scottdale, Pa.: Serendipity House, 1972), p. 23.

CHAPTER SIX

[1] Grand Rapids: Zondervan Publishing House, 1966.

[2] Ibid., pp. 95, 96.

[3] Rosalind Rinker, *Conversational Prayer* (Waco, Tex.: Word Books, 1970); *Prayer: Conversing With God* (Grand Rapids: Zondervan Publishing House) and a prayer workshop for the latter (Zondervan, 1973).

CHAPTER EIGHT

[1] William Barclay, *Letters to the Galatians and Ephesians* (Edinburgh: St. Andrew Press, 1954), p. 78.

[2] Ibid.

[3] For information on "mortal sin," see Hebrews 6:4-6; Matthew 12:31; and Mark 3:28.

[4] William Barclay, *The Gospel of Luke – The Daily Study Bible* (Edinburgh: St. Andrew Press, 3rd ed., 1956), pp. 9ff.

CHAPTER NINE

[1] See bibliography in back of this book.

Bibliography

I. Bible Study

A. Understanding the Bible

1. Bernhard W. Anderson, *Understanding the Old Testament.* Englewood Cliffs, N.J.: Prentice-Hall, Inc., 1957.
2. ———, *The Unfolding Drama of the Bible.* New York: National Board of YMCAs, Association Press, 1957.
3. William Barclay, *The Daily Study Bible,* 18 volumes. Edinburgh: St. Andrew Press.
4. ———, *The Mind of St. Paul.* New York: Harper & Brothers, 1958.
5. Robert McAfee Brown, *The Bible Speaks to You.* Philadelphia: Westminster Press, 1955.
6. Suzanne de Dietrich, *Discovering the Bible.* Nashville: Source Publishers, 1953.
7. Floyd V. Filson, *Opening the New Testament.* Englewood Cliffs, N.J.: Prentice-Hall, Inc., 1957.
8. Howard Clark Kee and Franklin W. Young, *Understanding the New Testament.* Englewood Cliffs, N.J.: Prentice-Hall, Inc., 1957.
9. William Neil, *The Plain Man Looks at the Bible.* London: Fontana Books, 1956.
10. ———, *The Rediscovery of the Bible.* London: Hodder & Stoughton, 1954.
11. *The New Bible Commentary,* ed. F. Davidson. Grand Rapids: W. B. Eerdmans Publishing Co., 1956.

B. Bible Study Dynamics

1. *Chart for Adventure.* Methods of Bible study. Edinburgh: Church of Scotland Youth Committee, 1962.
2. Winnie Christensen, *Caught With My Mouth Open.* Wheaton, Ill.: Harold Shaw Publishers, 1969.
3. Gladys Hunt, *It's Alive.* Wheaton, Ill.: Harold Shaw Publishers, 1971.
4. Lawrence O. Richards, *Creative Bible Study.* Grand Rapids: Zondervan Publishing House, 1971.
5. ———, *69 Ways To Start a Study Group and Keep It Growing.* Grand Rapids: Zondervan Publishing House, 1973.

C. Bible Study Materials

1. Walden Howard, *52 Weeks With the Bible*. Waco, Tex.: Faith at Work Publishers, 1965.
2. ———, *Group Encounters With the Bible*. Waco, Tex.: Faith at Work Publishers, 1967.
3. Catherine Schell and Marilyn Kunz, *Neighborhood Bible Studies*. Studies available in both Old and New Testaments. Excellent manual for conducting discussion-type Bible study. Available from Box 222, Dobbs Ferry, NY 10522.
4. *Ten Basic Steps Toward Christian Maturity*. A series of eleven booklets of topical studies related to the Christian life and experience. Order from Campus Crusade for Christ International, Mail Order Dept., Arrowhead Springs, San Bernardino CA 92404.
5. Scripture Union publications. Daily Bible study materials for all age-groups. Aimed at encouraging personal Bible study. In the United States, order from Scripture Union, 1716 Spruce Street, Philadelphia, PA 19103. In Canada, order from Scripture Union, 2100 Lawrence Ave. E., Scarborough M1R 2Z7, Ontario.

D. Group Life

1. Philip A. Anderson, *Church Meetings That Matter*. Philadelphia: United Church Press, 1965.
2. Dietrich Bonhoeffer, *Life Together*. New York: Harper Brothers, 1954.
3. Lyman Coleman, *Serendipity Books*. A series of programs for small-group use. Exciting materials to work with and excellent resources for anyone desiring to understand group processes. Order from Serendipity House, Order Dept. Box 461, Scottdale, PA 15683.
4. Leroy Judson Day, *Dynamic Christian Fellowship*. Valley Forge, Pa.: Judson Press, 1960.
5. Walden Howard, *Groups That Work*. Grand Rapids: Zondervan Publishing House, 1967.
6. Sara Little, *Learning Together in Christian Fellowship*. Richmond, Va.: John Knox Press, 1956.
7. Elizabeth O'Connor, *Journey Inward – Journey Outward*. New York: Harper & Row, Publishers, 1968.

8.———, *Eighth Day of Creation*. Waco, Tex.: Word Books, 1971.

9. Clyde H. Reid, *Groups Alive – Church Alive*. New York: Harper & Row, Publishers, 1969.

E. Prayer

1. Charles L. Allen, *Prayer Changes Things*. Old Tappan, N.J.: Fleming H. Revell, 1964.

2. O. Hallesby, *Prayer*. London: InterVarsity Fellowship, 1948.

3. Frank C. Laubach, *Prayer, the Mightiest Force in the World*. Old Tappan, N.J.: Fleming H. Revell, 1946.

4. Rosalind Rinker, *Communicating Love Through Prayer*. Grand Rapids: Zondervan Publishing House, 1966.

5. ———, *Prayer – Conversing With God*. Grand Rapids: Zondervan Publishing House, 1959.

6. ———, *Prayer – Conversing With God Prayer Workshop*. Grand Rapids: Zondervan Publishing House, 1973.

7. ———, *Praying Together*. Grand Rapids: Zondervan Publishing House, 1968.

8. ———, *Conversational Prayer* (formerly published as *Teaching Conversational Prayer*). Waco, Tex.: Word Books, 1970.